THE SIMON AND SCHUSTER ILLUSTRATED ENCYCLOPEDIA

PREHISTORIC WORLD

BY MICHAEL BENTON

LITTLE SIMON
PUBLISHED BY SIMON & SCHUSTER, INC.
NEW YORK

Copyright © 1987 by Grisewood & Dempsey Ltd

All rights reserved including the right of reproduction in whole or in part in any form
Published by Little Simon
A Division of Simon & Schuster, Inc.
Simon & Schuster Building
Rockefeller Center
1230 Avenue of the Americas
New York, New York 10020
Originally published in Great Britain by Grisewood & Dempsey Ltd., 1987
LITTLE SIMON and colophon are trademarks of Simon & Schuster, Inc.
Manufactured in Hong Kong
Printed and Bound by South China Printing Company
10 9 8 7 6 5 4 3 2 1
Library of Congress Cataloging in Publication Data

Benton, Michael.
    Prehistoric world.

    (The Simon and Schuster illustrated encyclopedia)
    "A Little Simon book."
    Summary: Discusses prehistoric life from the appearance of the first tiny plants to the first people.
    Includes index.
    1. Paleontology — Juvenile literature. 2. Fossil man — Juvenile literature. [1. Paleontology. 2. Prehistoric animals. 3. Man, Prehistoric. 4. Fossils] I. Title. II. Series.
QE714.5.B46   1988   560
87-20475
ISBN 0-671-64492-0

Contents

Introduction

Life on earth has not always been the same as it is today. The familiar plants and animals that we see around us have changed greatly since life first began, millions of years ago. If you had a time machine that allowed you to travel backward in time, you could see how these changes took place.

As you went backward in time, the plants and animals would begin to look less and less like the ones we know today. You might stop first in Stone Age times. There you would see early human beings wearing animal skins and living in caves. There would also be many animals that no longer exist — mammoths, giant wolves, cave bears, and saber-toothed cats. But most of the plants and animals would be very like those living today — pine and oak trees, mice, reindeer, horses, and so on.

Stone Age people hunted animals such as rabbits and deer for food, using spears and arrows with sharp heads made from stone. They lived and slept in caves, and used animal skins to keep them warm. This is a scene that you might have seen in Europe or North America ten thousand years ago.

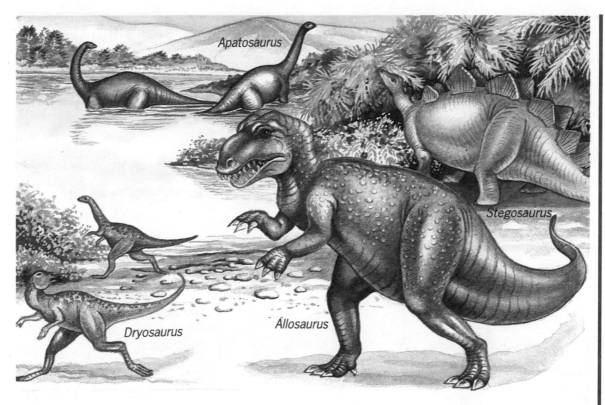

Apatosaurus

Stegosaurus

Dryosaurus

Allosaurus

If you jumped even further back in time, the world would seem very different indeed. Let us go back to the age when dinosaurs lived on the earth. Now there are no humans alive at all. The land is covered with strange, primitive-looking trees. Many different kinds of dinosaurs can be seen — the giant *Apatosaurus* moves slowly around a lake; *Stegosaurus*, with a line of bony plates down its back, munches some leaves; the giant meat-eater *Allosaurus* moves menacingly toward a herd of smaller two-legged plant-eaters called *Dryosaurus*. You would have to hunt around very carefully to find any plant or animal in this scene that still survives today.

Let us go back before the age of the dinosaurs to the earth of 500 million years ago. Here there are no animals or plants on land at all. If you could travel down to the sea bed, you would see some very strange animals indeed — some look like corals, others like shellfish, others like giant wood lice. None of these creatures is alive today.

Clues to the past

How do we know what life was like on earth hundreds of millions of years ago? The answer lies in the study of **fossils**. Fossils are the remains of ancient plants and animals that have been preserved in ancient rocks. They can tell us what the animals looked like, even what they ate, how fast they ran, and what their babies were like! This book follows the story of how scientists have studied the **prehistoric** world, and what they have found out about the history of life.

When dinosaurs ruled the earth there were no human beings alive at all. Even the plants and trees looked very different from modern ones.

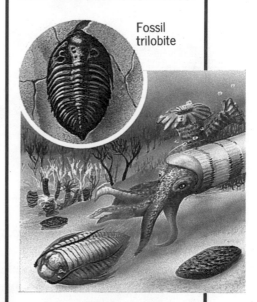

Fossil trilobite

The fossil shown at the top of the picture is a trilobite from 400-million-year-old rocks. This animal lived on the sea bed long before human beings or even dinosaurs were around.

7

1. Learning about the Past

Early ideas

The history of life is like a fascinating detective story. The "evidence" for the story comes from fossils, and these are not always easy to understand. In fact, it has taken scientists a long time to piece together the different important parts of the history.

Xenophanes was puzzled to find fossils of fish and sea-shells in rocks a long way from the sea. He did not realize that the sea had once covered Greece.

Strange rocks

In Ancient Greece, many years before the birth of Christ, people sometimes picked up bones that seemed to be preserved in the rock. These were very hard to explain. About 600 years before Christ, a Greek scientist called Xenophanes found fossils of fish and seashells in the rocks. They were a long way from the sea, and he could not understand how they had got there.

Many early scientists puzzled over this problem. Were the fossils just strange pieces of rock, and not really the remains of fish and shellfish at all? Had they been carried from the sea up into the hills by wandering people — the remains of their lunches?

Understanding the clues

It was the great Italian scientist Leonardo da Vinci who found the answer, in the late 15th century. The remains of fish and shellfish could now be found on land because the seas had once covered those areas in former times. Leonardo also worked out how these fossils had been formed. He argued that when the fish and shellfish had died, they had fallen to the bottom of the sea. There they were buried by the mud, and their flesh rotted away. Over a long period of time the mud hardened into rock and the hard bones and shells became fossils.

Over the next two hundred years, scientists continued to argue about what fossils were. A Danish scientist called Steno wrote an important book in the 17th century about the fossil teeth of sharks. He had discovered that shark's teeth were common as fossils, and that some sharks of the past were much larger than living ones.

The British scientist Robert Plot also studied fossils in the 17th century. He is famous for having found the first bone of a dinosaur, although he did not know it at the time. He thought it might have come from an elephant, or from a giant human being. We can tell now that it was part of the thigh bone of the dinosaur *Megalosaurus*.

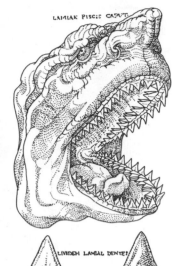
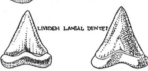

Steno's strange-looking picture of a shark's head and fossil shark's teeth. He showed that the fossil teeth were exactly the same as the teeth of a modern shark.

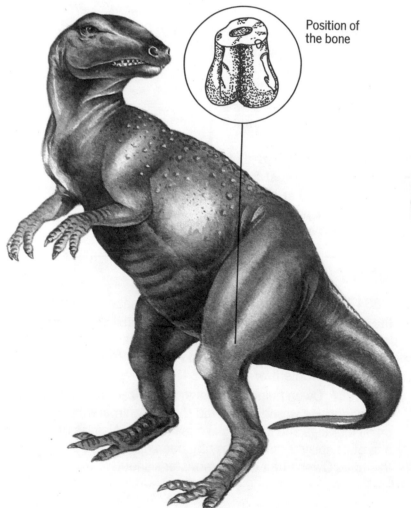

Position of the bone

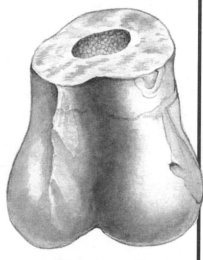

The first picture of a dinosaur bone came from a book printed in 1676. It is the end of a thigh bone of the meat-eating dinosaur Megalosaurus. Plot thought it came from an elephant, or a giant human.

9

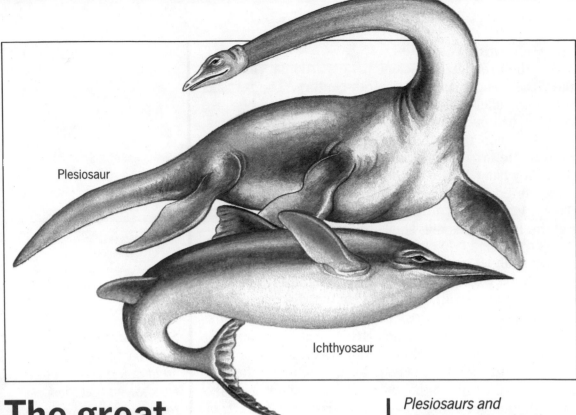

Plesiosaur

Ichthyosaur

The great fossil hunters

By 1800, scientists had collected fossil bones from many parts of the world. Among them were the teeth, tusks, and bones of giant fossil elephants from North America and Europe. These did not seem to be very ancient, and were quite easy to explain. But other, stranger fossil skeletons had also been found, and these were much more puzzling.

On the coasts of the south of England and of Yorkshire in the northeast, the local people used to see great bones on the shore. The waves of the sea battered at the cliffs and gradually wore away at the rock. After great storms, the **skeletons** of ancient crocodiles and sea monsters

Plesiosaurs and ichthyosaurs lived in the sea during the age of the dinosaurs. Fossil skeletons of both animals were well known by about 1820.

SIR RICHARD OWEN

(1804-1892) was a leading expert on dinosaurs. He was the first to realize that dinosaurs were not just giant lizards, but an important group of animals that had completely died out. He invented the name *Dinosauria*, meaning "terrible lizards," in 1841.

In 1851, Owen helped to design a life-sized model of *Iguanodon*. He wrongly believed that the animal walked on all four legs and looked like a giant rhino. Also, as only one of its spiky fossil thumbs had been discovered at this time, Owen put it on the monster's snout!

Sir Richard Owen's model of Iguanodon *was built in 1851 for the Great Exhibition in London. A special dinner, attended by many great scientists, was held inside the model before it was set up (top picture). The bottom picture shows how modern scientists think* Iguanodon *looked.*

were uncovered. Some of these sea monsters had long, snakelike necks and large paddles. They were called **plesiosaurs**. Others had fishlike bodies and long snouts lined with sharp teeth. These were called **ichthyosaurs**. The scientists in London paid large sums of money for these rare and remarkable fossil skeletons. They could see that England had once been the home of huge, dragonlike monsters.

The first dinosaurs

In the 1820s, new bones were dug up inland in the south of England, and some scientists came to realize that there had also been "dragons" on land at the same time as the ichthyosaurs and plesiosaurs lived in the seas. The bones of a large reptile were brought to William Buckland, the professor of geology at Oxford University, in 1818. The most interesting bone was part of a jaw with several long sharp teeth like steak knives. Buckland named the animal *Megalosaurus* in 1824, although he was not really sure what kind of creature it was.

The second dinosaur to be named was found in Sussex in the south of England in 1822. Mary Ann Mantell was out walking along a country road when she spotted two large fossil teeth. She showed them to her husband, Doctor Gideon Mantell, who studied them. More bones were later found nearby, and in 1825 he named his giant "lizard" *Iguanodon*. Gradually, scientists realized that the bones had come from a very strange and unfamiliar group of animals indeed — the "dinosaurs." Many more skeletons of *Iguanodon* were found in England, and by 1850 it was a very famous dinosaur.

11

Bone Wars in the West

By about 1870, dinosaur skeletons had been dug up in many parts of the world, and many different **species** were known. Interest began to shift from Europe to North America as the new continent was opened up by the explorers. Stories of great dinosaur graveyards in the West came back to the scientists in New York and the eastern states.

This exciting news set off the great dinosaur bone rush of the late 19th century. Two scientists, Edward Cope and Othniel Marsh, brought back hundreds of tons of bones of the biggest dinosaurs anyone had ever seen.

Cope and Marsh began collecting fossils together, but by 1869 rivalry had soured their friendship. They became sworn enemies, and the fierce battle for bones continued until Cope's death in 1897.

In 1877, Arthur Lakes, a schoolteacher who was traveling in Colorado, found some giant bones. On receiving them, Marsh immediately paid Lakes $100 to keep the discovery a secret and to continue collecting. Meanwhile, another schoolteacher, O.W. Lucas, found similar large bones nearby and sent these to Cope. Cope paid Lucas to collect bones for him. The race was on to find new species of dinosaurs.

Edward Cope (above) and Othniel Marsh (below, middle of back row) were great rivals in the late 1800s. Their teams of collectors often armed themselves like gunfighters in case of an attack from unfriendly Indians!

The early collectors employed by Marsh and Cope worked in extreme difficulties. They had to bring in all their supplies on horseback and were forced to carry the huge bones and skeletons long distances to the nearest railroads. Marsh and Cope paid the collectors to work all year round, even when it was snowing. There were also hostile Indians to be coped with. It is said that the workmen employed by Cope and Marsh to dig up the Colorado dinosaurs even fought with each other to get the best bones.

As the huge crates of bones reached the East, Cope and Marsh hurried to unpack them. They quickly cleaned the rock from the bones and had detailed drawings made. Often Cope and Marsh received skeletons of the same new species of dinosaur at the same time. They each rushed to publish their discovery before the other, and this often meant that both scientists gave different names to the same animal. This made them hate each other all the more.

The great dinosaur bone rush of the late 19th century increased our knowledge of dinosaurs enormously. Between them, Cope and Marsh discovered dozens of new dinosaur species, including the well-known *Allosaurus, Apatosaurus (Brontosaurus), Camarasaurus, Camptosaurus, Coelophysis, Diplodocus, Stegosaurus,* and *Triceratops.*

Dinosaurs are dug up in many parts of the world today. This is still a very long and hard job. It may take weeks to carefully uncover the whole skeleton, and each bone must be protected from damage.

13

Studying fossils

Scientists have learned about prehistoric life by studying fossils. Fossils are the remains of plants and animals that once lived. Fossils can be very ancient, and they are usually turned into rock in some way. Many common fossils can be very beautiful objects that show a great deal of fine detail, like fossil shells with surface patterns, whole insects trapped in amber, or skeletons of tiny fish preserved in fine mud.

Not every plant or animal that lives will become a fossil. Some animals, such as worms and jellyfish, have no hard parts at all. This means that when they die, and their flesh rots away, there is nothing left to form a fossil. The commonest fossils are the shells or bones of animals, or the tough outer skins of plants.

Forming fossils

Fossils are found in rocks such as sandstones, mudstones, and limestones that have hardened over long periods of time from sands or muds. Perhaps the most fascinating fossils are those of the dinosaurs, so let us follow the story of how one dinosaur became a fossil.

A long-necked plant-eating dinosaur of the early Jurassic period (200 million years ago) dies beside a riverbank. Its body is washed into the river and is covered by

①

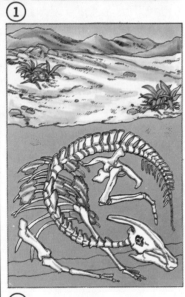
②

③

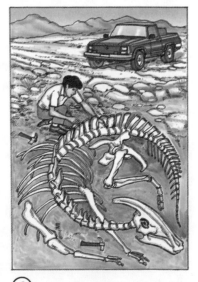
④

A dinosaur dies by the side of a river, and its body is washed away (1). The flesh rots, leaving only a skeleton, and the bones are covered by sand (2).

Over thousands of years, the skeleton is buried under more layers of sand and mud that harden into rock (3). The bones turn into fossils.

Many millions of years later, the fossil skeleton is uncovered by the wearing-down action of the wind and water. A scientist finds the skeleton (4).

sand. The flesh rots away, leaving the bony skeleton. Over many thousands of years, the river brings down many more layers of sand and mud that are dumped on top of the skeleton. Chemicals may seep into the bones as the rock hardens, and the bones may become much harder and heavier. They have become fossils.

Studying the fossils

Many millions of years later, the earth has changed. The old river-bottom rocks are worn away, and the fossilized dinosaur skeleton is uncovered. A scientist comes by one day exploring for fossils. He spots the dinosaur skeleton, and brings out a team to dig it up. It may take as many as ten people to dig up a single dinosaur skeleton. They often have to remove tons of rock that lie above, and then they have to use small drills and chisels to clean up the bones. The smallest slip could destroy a valuable fossil find! After weeks of careful digging, the bones have to be wrapped up in plaster to protect them. They are taken back to the museum by truck or train.

In the museum laboratory, the bones are carefully cleaned up and repaired. If the skeleton is a good one, it may be set up in a lifelike pose in the museum. Scientists then study the skeleton and other fossils to work out what life was like in the early Jurassic when that dinosaur was alive.

This insect has been trapped in fossilized tree resin (amber) for about 30 million years. Even the veins of the wings can still be clearly seen.

⑤

A team of scientists carefully uncovers the whole skeleton, chipping the rock away bit by bit. It has to be wrapped in plaster for protection (5).

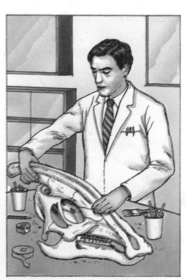

⑥

Back in the laboratory, the bones are carefully cleaned up and repaired. This can take many months, since it has to be done very slowly (6).

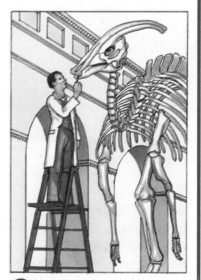

⑦

Experts in museums can rebuild whole skeletons from fossil bones (7). Such skeletons tell scientists many things about how the dinosaur lived.

Scenes from the past

Scientists try to understand as much as possible about the life of the past. They can learn a great deal by looking at a single dinosaur skeleton. They can work out how it walked and ran by looking at its legs. They can discover what it ate by examining its teeth. However, even more can be learned by looking at the rocks that surrounded the skeleton, and by studying the other fossils that were found with it.

Scientists who study rocks are called **geologists**. They can find out whether the dinosaur died beside a river, or beside the sea, by looking at the rocks. For example, it may be possible to find old river channels or the shape of an ancient lake. Sometimes, geologists even find fossil mud cracks or sand ripples that look just like the markings on a modern beach. They can even work out how hot or cold the climate was, and how long ago the dinosaur lived.

Fossil experts, or **paleontologists**, can then examine all the fossilized remains in the same rock. There could well be other skeletons of smaller animals, shells, or

Below: a fossil of a pollen grain from Cretaceous rocks, seen under the microscope. Tiny fossils like this can be very common in certain rocks, and they allow paleontologists to identify what plants were present.

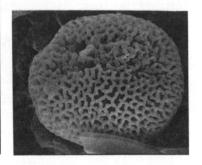

Above: a beautifully preserved fossil leaf from a Cretaceous plane tree. All that remains is a thin film of carbon on the surface of the rock, yet the veins of the leaf can still be clearly seen.

Below: a scene from the Cretaceous period (about 100 million years ago) in Alberta, Canada. Every plant and animal shown here is based on fossils that have been found together in the same rocks. This gives a detailed picture of life at this time.

leaves of plants. It is important to know as much as possible about all these other fossils in order to get a complete picture of what life was really like at the time.

Ancient life in Alberta

In Alberta, Canada, many dinosaurs have been found in rocks that are 70 million years old. These include the horn-faced plant-eater *Triceratops*, the curious duck-billed *Parasaurolophus* and *Corythosaurus*, and the small, agile meat-eating dinosaur *Stenonychosaurus*.

The rocks also contain skeletons of frogs, lizards, birds, the flying reptiles called **pterosaurs**, and small shrewlike **mammals**. There are also the remains of lake-living shellfish, delicate fossils of flies and beetles, and leaves of trees and smaller plants.

The rocks tell us that the climate was warm, and that there were broad lakes and rivers lying quite near to an ancient sea that ran up the middle of North America at that time. There were large forests that provided plenty of food for the plant-eating dinosaurs. The meat-eating *Stenonychosaurus* may have fed on frogs, lizards, and mammals since it was too small to attack most of the plant-eating dinosaurs.

Above: the skull of the horned dinosaur Triceratops, *which lived in Cretaceous times.* Triceratops *is also shown in the picture on the left.*

17

How old is the earth?

By 1750, most scientists had come to accept that fossils were the remains of plants and animals that had once lived. However, they still did not understand how old the earth really was.

The most accurate estimate for the age of the earth had been made in 1650 by James Ussher, the Archbishop of Armagh in Ireland. He studied the Bible closely, and added together the ages of all of the main characters. He concluded that the earth had been created in the year 4004 B.C. John Lightfoot of Cambridge University in England then worked out that this great event had taken place at 9 A.M. on Sunday, October 26, in 4004 B.C.!

During the next two hundred years, scientists began to doubt this figure. The geologists in particular could just not accept that the history of the earth had taken place in only 6,000 years. The early geologists looked at the great thicknesses of rock in cliffs and quarries and argued that these must have taken huge amounts of time to be laid down.

James Hutton, a Scottish geologist, spent many years looking at rock formations. His findings provided evidence that the earth was very ancient. He was thinking not in thousands of years, but in *millions*. After 1800, most scientists accepted that **geological time** (the age of the earth and of all its rock formations) was immense.

James Hutton (1726-1797) proved that the earth was millions of years old. Some rock formations showed how the layers had been tilted up and that more rock had then been laid down on top. This must have taken a huge amount of time.

GEORGES CUVIER (1769-1832)

proved that many animals, such as mammoths and mastodons, had become extinct. The scene on the right shows a great dig for a mastodon skeleton in 1802.

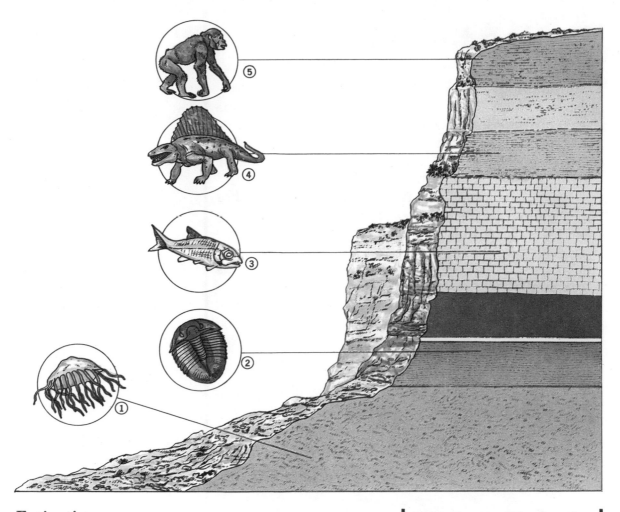

Extinction

Until about 1800, most scientists thought that the plants and animals whose remains had been found were all still living. Much of the world at that time was not very well known. Explorers kept bringing back new and unusual plants and animals from the jungles of Africa and South America, and from the plains of Australia. It was easy to look at an unusual fossil and say that the animal or plant could still be found in some unexplored part of the world.

During the 1700s, giant teeth and bones of elephant-like animals had been found in many parts of Europe and North America. At first, the scientists said that these strange elephants probably still lived in the jungle somewhere. However, as more and more fossil bones of strange giant animals turned up, it became harder to believe that explorers had not seen them. These early elephants were called mammoths and mastodons. Georges Cuvier, a famous French scientist, argued that the animals had died out, or become **extinct**. This was quite a shocking idea for many people at the time, since it seemed to suggest that God had made a mistake. If all living things were specially created, why should any of them become extinct? However, the evidence was so strong that scientists came to accept Cuvier's idea.

This cutaway of the Grand Canyon in Arizona shows the great thicknesses of rock that have been laid down in different periods (see page 21). At the bottom are Precambrian rocks (1), followed by Cambrian (2), Carboniferous (3), Permian (4), and Miocene rocks (5). These rocks cover about 700 million years, and the history of life is recorded in typical fossils of each period.

Dating the past

Geologists divide up the history of the earth into a number of geological periods. These are listed in the diagram on the opposite page. Different plants and animals lived in different periods. The older geological periods contain simpler and more ancient types of plants and animals than the more recent ones.

Scientists date these periods in millions of years. For example, we know from fossil findings in the rocks that the earliest human beings lived about five million years ago. The dinosaurs appeared about 215 million years ago, and they died out 65 million years ago. The earth was formed about 4,600 million years ago.

These amounts of time are huge. It is very difficult to picture how long one million years is, let alone 4,600 million. Written records of human history go back a few thousand years, but it is very hard to imagine the vast amount of time that stretches back before this.

Geological time in millions of years is measured by chemical means. Over very long periods of time, the materials in certain kinds of rocks change into others. Geologists can measure how much the materials have changed, and then use this information to find the age of the rock in millions of years.

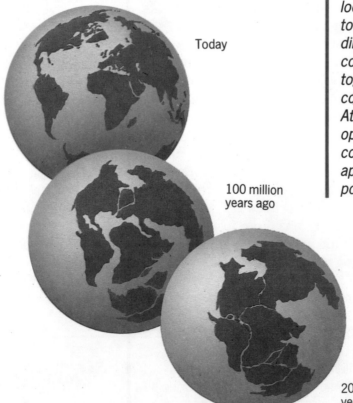

Today

100 million years ago

200 million years ago

The earth has not always looked the same as it does today. During the age of the dinosaurs, most of the continents were joined together as a single large continent. Since then, the Atlantic Ocean has gradually opened up, and the continents have moved apart to their present positions.

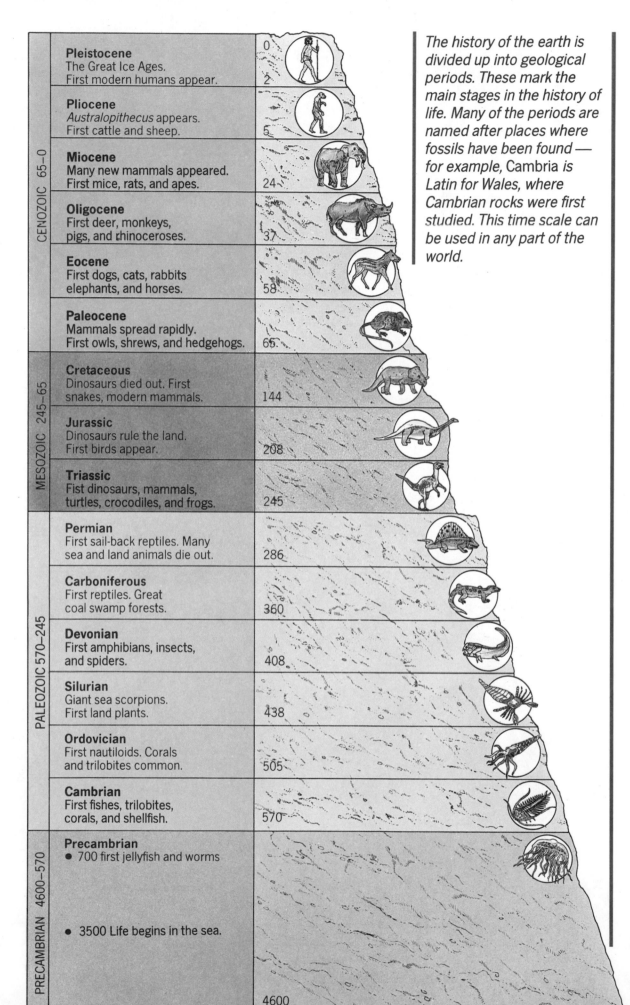

The history of the earth is divided up into geological periods. These mark the main stages in the history of life. Many of the periods are named after places where fossils have been found — for example, *Cambria* is Latin for Wales, where Cambrian rocks were first studied. This time scale can be used in any part of the world.

CENOZOIC 65–0

Pleistocene
The Great Ice Ages.
First modern humans appear.
0
2

Pliocene
Australopithecus appears.
First cattle and sheep.
5

Miocene
Many new mammals appeared.
First mice, rats, and apes.
24

Oligocene
First deer, monkeys,
pigs, and rhinoceroses.
37

Eocene
First dogs, cats, rabbits
elephants, and horses.
58

Paleocene
Mammals spread rapidly.
First owls, shrews, and hedgehogs.
65

MESOZOIC 245–65

Cretaceous
Dinosaurs died out. First
snakes, modern mammals.
144

Jurassic
Dinosaurs rule the land.
First birds appear.
208

Triassic
Fist dinosaurs, mammals,
turtles, crocodiles, and frogs.
245

PALEOZOIC 570–245

Permian
First sail-back reptiles. Many
sea and land animals die out.
286

Carboniferous
First reptiles. Great
coal swamp forests.
360

Devonian
First amphibians, insects,
and spiders.
408

Silurian
Giant sea scorpions.
First land plants.
438

Ordovician
First nautiloids. Corals
and trilobites common.
505

Cambrian
First fishes, trilobites,
corals, and shellfish.
570

PRECAMBRIAN 4600–570

Precambrian
● 700 first jellyfish and worms

● 3500 Life begins in the sea.

4600

The changing world

Fossils show us clearly that life has changed, or **evolved**, over many millions of years. Small changes may happen even in a few hundred years, and over millions of years these can add up to very large changes indeed.

Most scientists believe that plants and animals have evolved in order to survive in a changing world. For example, the first giraffe might have been an early deer that just happened to have a slightly longer neck than usual. It could reach higher up into the trees than any other deer, and it found it easier to live if food was in short supply. Its babies would all have longer necks, because baby animals always look like their parents. Eventually we have the giraffes of today that have evolved such long necks over the past 20 million years that they seem to be nothing like deer at all!

Other species of animal have died out altogether. At certain times in the history of the earth, we now know that whole groups of animals and plants died out at the same time. This is called **mass extinction**.

Since the first primitive form arose about 3,500 million years ago, many different plants and animals have evolved. Here the major groups are shown by different color bands — green for plants, fungi (mushrooms and toadstools), and the single-celled bacteria and blue-green algae; blue for animals without backbones and red for animals with backbones.

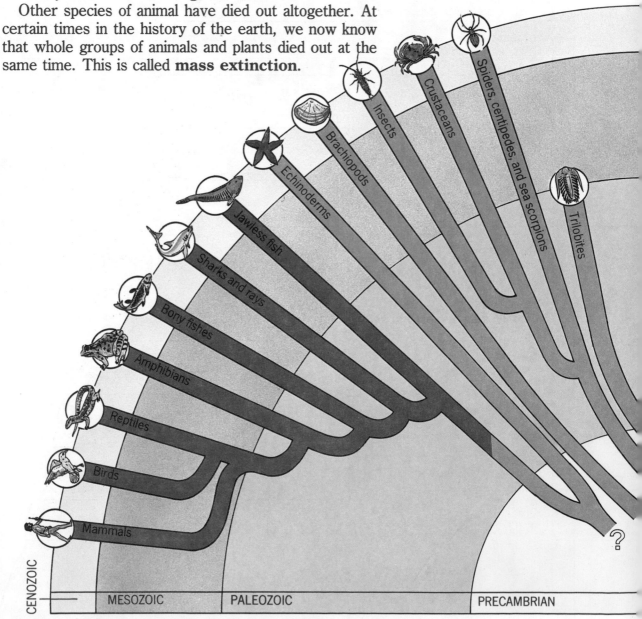

Spiders, centipedes, and sea scorpions

Crustaceans

Insects

Brachiopods

Echinoderms

Jawless fish

Sharks and rays

Bony fishes

Amphibians

Reptiles

Birds

Mammals

Trilobites

CENOZOIC | MESOZOIC | PALEOZOIC | PRECAMBRIAN

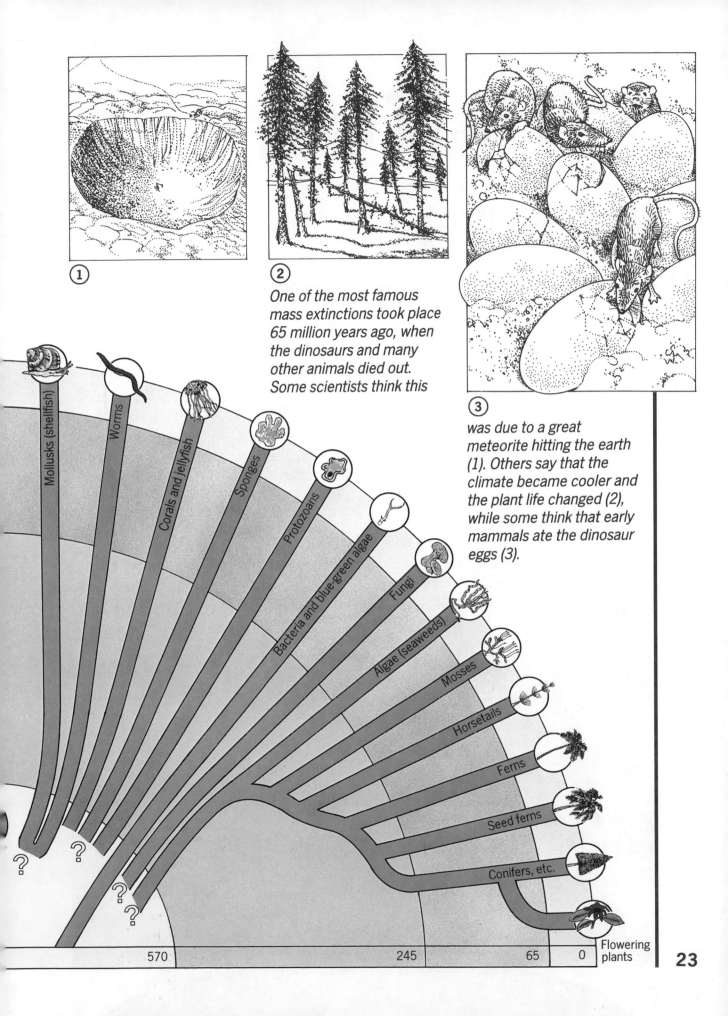

① ②

One of the most famous mass extinctions took place 65 million years ago, when the dinosaurs and many other animals died out. Some scientists think this

③

was due to a great meteorite hitting the earth (1). Others say that the climate became cooler and the plant life changed (2), while some think that early mammals ate the dinosaur eggs (3).

Mollusks (shellfish)

Worms

Corals and jellyfish

Sponges

Protozoans

Bacteria and blue-green algae

Fungi

Algae (seaweeds)

Mosses

Horsetails

Ferns

Seed ferns

Conifers, etc.

Flowering plants

570   245   65   0

2. The Birth of Life

How life began

To begin with, there was no life on earth at all. For hundreds of millions of years, the earth was far too hot for anything to survive. Geologists believe that the earth formed as a great ball of molten rock, and that it took about a billion years to cool down enough for a solid crust to form on the outside.

Scientists think that life began 3,500 million years ago, long after the earth had first formed. The first living

Scientists believe that the earth formed from a molten ball of rock. Great lightning storms raged over the surface, and volcanoes were very common everywhere. It took many millions of years to cool.

things were probably very simple tiny creatures that could only have been seen under a microscope. They might have been like the **bacteria** we know today. Bacteria are single **cells** — just small bags of living chemicals that can eat and divide to form new bacteria.

Experiments have been carried out to show how life began in the early seas. Mixtures of simple chemicals were placed in a large glass jar, and electrical sparks were sent through it. The sparks were supposed to represent lightning, which was probably very common on the early earth. After a week or so, the scientists found that complex chemicals had formed in the glass jar. These chemicals were just like the chemicals that are found in simple living cells.

Scientists believe that this is how life first began in the ancient seas. Lightning struck the surface of the sea, and this led to the formation of complex chemicals. Eventually, the right chemicals arose and gave birth to the first simple living creatures.

There are some fossils of these very early simple creatures, but most of them were so tiny that they are not often found in the ancient rocks. However, some special types of early fossils, called **stromatolites**, do tell us a great deal about the early forms of life. Stromatolites are mounds formed from mud and layers of simple living cells. They grow to about the size of a large cabbage, and they can still be found today. Mosses have been found in rocks up to 3,500 million years old, so we can tell that simple life must have existed then.

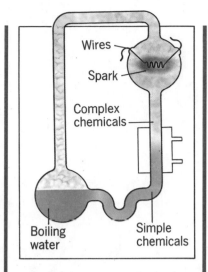

An experiment that showed how life might have begun. Electrical sparks were passed through a glass jar containing the same simple chemicals that were found in ancient seas. Complex lifelike chemicals were formed after a few days.

STROMATOLITES

A layer of cells forms on the seabed (1). After a while, it may be covered by mud, and the cells form a new layer on top (2). Eventually the layers build up into a mound (3).

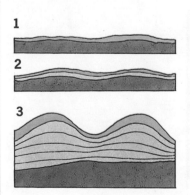

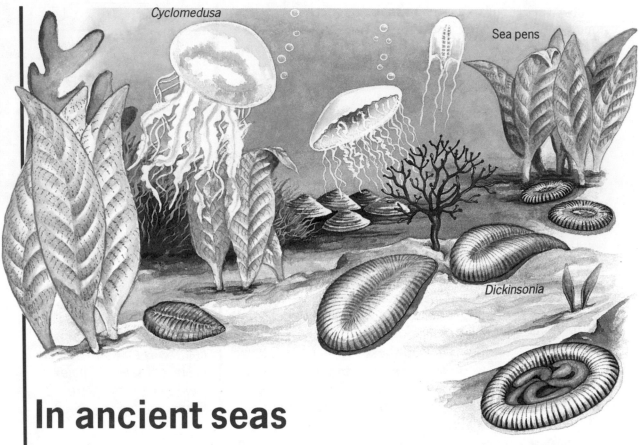

Cyclomedusa

Sea pens

Dickinsonia

In ancient seas

For many hundreds of millions of years, life in the sea remained very simple. The only creatures were tiny single-celled forms that lived near the top of the water. Then, about 680 million years ago, larger and more complex types of plants and animals appeared in the seas. These were each made up from many cells, as we are ourselves.

The most famous of these early many-celled animals were found at Ediacara in Australia. Paleontologists split open the thin slabs of brown mudstone and found fossils of a number of different animals. There were jellyfish, worms, corallike animals, and others. The amazing thing about these fossils is that most of them are the remains of soft-bodied animals — it is very unusual for a worm or a jellyfish to be turned into a fossil, since they do not have any hard parts.

The Ediacara jellyfish called *Cyclomedusa* probably swam about and fed on small pieces of food in the water. Most of the other animals lived on the seabed. The worms, like *Dickinsonia*, were broad flat creatures that plowed through the mud and fed on small pieces of buried food.

Cambrian life
The Ediacara animals lived near the end of Precambrian times. During the next geological period, the Cambrian,

The fossils found in Ediacara in Australia show some of the first animals that ever lived on the earth. These include the jellyfish Cyclomedusa, some sea pens, and the flat worm Dickinsonia.

many new sea creatures appeared. Many of these had hard parts — shells or tough outer skeletons – and fossils became much commoner all over the world from this time onward.

Some of the commonest Cambrian fossils are a special group of shellfish called the **brachiopods**. There are still a few living brachiopods, but they are very rare and quite different from the more common shellfish of today, such as mussels and clams. Brachiopods lived near the sea-bed, and usually fixed themselves to the bottom by a short stalk.

Creatures of the Burgess Shale
We have learned about the animals of the Cambrian seas in great detail from a famous rock formation in Canada called the Burgess Shale. Here, as at Ediacara, fossils of soft-bodied animals are found. There were various kinds of worms, corals, and sponges, and a number of animals with legs. Some of these were very strange indeed. *Hallucigenia* had seven pairs of stiff spines underneath, and seven flexible arms along its back. *Opabinia* had five large eyes and a long flexible trunk at the front, with claws on the end for picking up food. Some of these animals really look like creatures from another planet!

A section through a modern brachiopod showing the stalk and the feeding tentacles. Brachiopods are rare today, but they were the most common shellfish in Cambrian times.

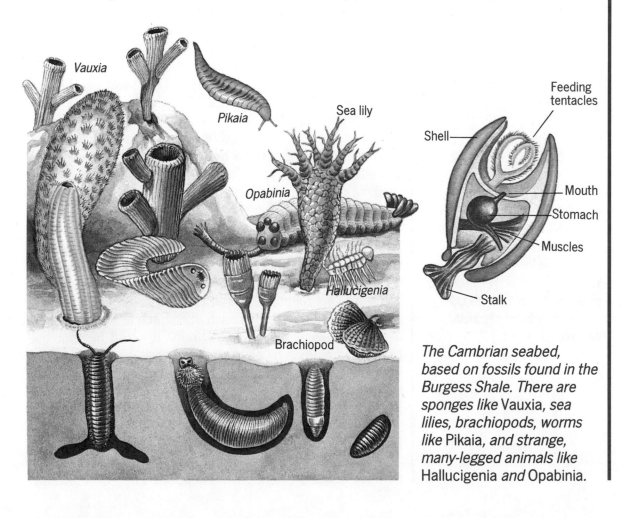

The Cambrian seabed, based on fossils found in the Burgess Shale. There are sponges like Vauxia, *sea lilies, brachiopods, worms like* Pikaia, *and strange, many-legged animals like* Hallucigenia *and* Opabinia.

A Silurian coral reef in the warm waters of Europe or North America. The reef is made up from horn corals, colonial corals, and sea lilies. Among the animals that hunted for food in the waters of the coral reef was the fierce sea scorpion Pterygotus, which could grow up to 6½ feet long.

Horn coral

Nautiloid

Colonial coral

Sea lily

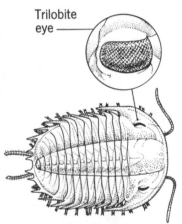

Trilobite eye

Trilobites had many legs, one under each section of their bodies, and looked rather like wood lice do today. They had remarkable eyes that were made up from dozens of separate lenses.

One of the most important groups of animals in these early seas were the **trilobites**. These had a tough skeleton on the outside, just like their distant living relatives, the crabs, lobsters, spiders, and insects.

Trilobites were very active creatures. They could run about on the seabed quite fast, and they could also use their many legs for swimming. They probably fed on particles of food that they found in the mud, or even on other small animals.

One of the most remarkable things about trilobites was their eyes. These are the first eyes that ever existed on the earth, and we can work out just how trilobites saw their world 500 million years ago! The eyes of trilobites were very large, ball-like structures, just like the eyes of living flies. The trilobite could look forward, sideways, backward, and upward at the same time. The surface of the eye was divided up into a honeycomblike pattern consisting of dozens, even hundreds, of separate **lenses.** This meant that the trilobite saw many different pictures of its world with each eye. Each lens sent back a slightly different view to the brain. It could be that the trilobite actually saw all of those dozens of pictures, just like a great stack of separate TV screens. More probably, it was able to fuse the pictures together in its brain just as we fuse the pictures we see with our two eyes.

Life in a coral reef

The lovely, plantlike corals are actually small sea animals that live inside a tough outer skeleton. They first became

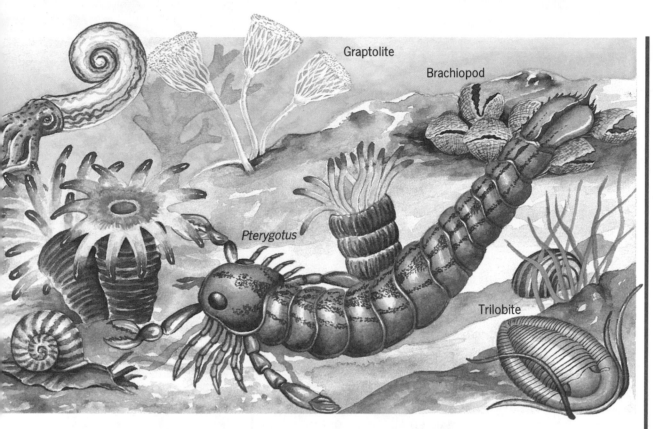

Graptolite

Brachiopod

Pterygotus

Trilobite

common in the Silurian, and built up great mounds on the seabed in shallow coastal regions. There were horn corals shaped like ice-cream cones, which were fixed to the seabed. The coral animal lived at the top, and stretched out its tentacles to feed on floating food in the water. There were also colonial corals that were made up by many tiny animals that built themselves a hard, stony outer skeleton. The colonial coral skeleton could be shaped like a baseball, a cabbage, or a pancake. The Silurian coral animals were probably brightly colored, just as modern corals are.

A whole variety of other animals lived in and around the coral reefs. There were sea lilies fixed to the seabed. Various types of shellfish and trilobites crept in and around the corals. Larger animals also hunted in the waters around the coral reefs. There were large **nautiloids**, relatives of the living octopus, and giant sea scorpions such as *Pterygotus*, which had strong claws to seize other animals.

The history of the earliest life in the sea. The first life was made up of simple bacterialike creatures and the stromatolite mounds. Then brachiopods and trilobites came on the scene in the Cambrian, followed by corals and sea scorpions in the Ordovician and Silurian.

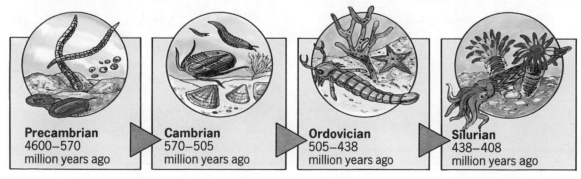

Precambrian
4600–570
million years ago

Cambrian
570–505
million years ago

Ordovician
505–438
million years ago

Silurian
438–408
million years ago

The story of fish

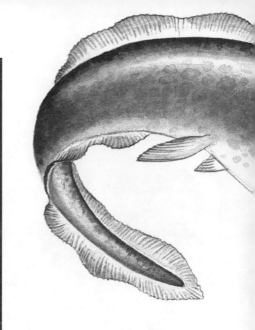

The Devonian period is sometimes called the Age of Fish, as these animals changed and became very numerous during this time. Most of these fish looked very different from the ones we know today.

Many were heavily armored, with great bony plates arranged like hard boxes over their heads. It has been suggested that these early fish were armed in this way as protection against giant sea scorpions like *Pterygotus*.

Many of the Devonian armored fish had no jaws. These are called **ostracoderms**, meaning "bony skin." An example is *Hemicyclaspis*, which had a rounded head shield with the eyes placed on top. The main paddles were just behind the head shield, and the rest of the body was covered with strips of bone so that the body could bend for swimming. *Hemicyclaspis* did not have a jaw, only a suckerlike mouth. This meant that it could not bite its food. It must have fed by plowing through the mud on the sea floor, and by sucking up small pieces of food. The ostracoderms might have given rise to the living jawless

Two early armored fish of the Devonian period. Hemicyclaspis *had a rounded head shield and lived near the seabed.* Pteraspis *was better adapted for swimming.*

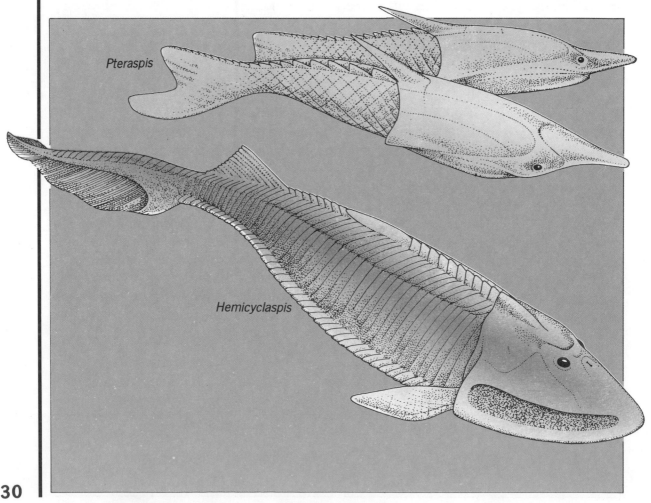

Pteraspis

Hemicyclaspis

Climatius

Cladoselache

Jamoytius

fish, the lampreys, but that is not certain. Lampreys are very different from ostracoderms since they have no armor.

Pteraspis was another ostracoderm. It had a longer, bullet-shaped head shield, and this suggests that it could probably swim quite fast. *Pteraspis* did not have such heavy scales on its tail, which also suggests that its body was more flexible for rapid swimming.

The first fish
The very earliest fish were not armored like the ostracoderms. They were small, wormlike creatures with a few fins that allowed them to swim. The important thing about these early fish is that they had a backbone, just like reptiles, birds, and human beings. Scientists are very interested in tracing how these backboned animals first evolved.

An important clue has come from studying some rare animals called sea squirts. Sea squirts look like floppy plastic bags fixed to the seabed. Like corals, they feed by picking up pieces of food that float their way. It seems impossible that these could be the ancestors of the fish and of all the other animals with backbones. However, the babies of sea squirts are very different. They do have a kind of backbone, and swim about in the sea using fins. Scientists now believe that the link between the animals without backbones and the first fish was the baby sea squirt.

A seabed scene from Devonian times showing different kinds of fish. There are some early sharks like Cladoselache and sharklike forms such as Climatius, as well as the primitive Jamoytius and a small relative of the great plated Dunkleosteus.

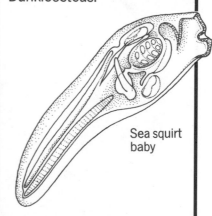

Sea squirt baby

A sea squirt baby. This strange creature is very fish-like, with a sort of backbone, and it is similar to the ancestor of the fish.

31

A fossil of the giant Devonian fish Dunkleosteus. *This massive placoderm lurked on the seabed, waiting for its prey to swim past. Smaller armored fish would have been helpless against its powerful, jagged jaws.*

Massive jaws

The first really giant fish also appeared in the Devonian period. Unlike the jawless ostracoderms, these fish were able to bite their food. They were still very strange-looking, and some of them had great plates of bone over their heads and bodies. Some, like *Bothriolepis*, had bony plates over their paddles. These are called **placoderms** meaning "platy skin."

The first really giant fish appeared in the Devonian period. This was a placoderm called *Dunkleosteus*. *Dunkleosteus* was up to 30 feet long — about as long as a bus — and it had a huge head that was the size of a car. The head was made from great bony plates, and the jaws were lined with sharp cutting bone plates. These were not teeth, but more like the blades on a giant pair of scissors. *Dunkleosteus* could easily have eaten any of the other Devonian fish simply by snipping them in two with its massive jaws.

The first sharks

Sharks first appeared in the Devonian period. The earliest sharks, such as *Cladoselache*, were not very large. *Cladoselache* was primitive, since it had its mouth right at the front of its head instead of tucked underneath as do modern sharks and rays (the flat-bodied relatives of sharks). At the same time, there were some smaller sharklike animals such as *Climatius* that had many spines and fins on their backs.

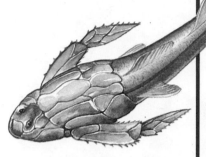

Bothriolepis *was a smaller relative of* Dunkleosteus. *It had bony plates covering its head region, and over the large crablike side paddles.*

The fossil record of sharks is not very good. Their skeletons are not made of bone, like other fish, but of the softer gristly material called cartilage. Often the only parts of a shark that are found as fossils are the teeth and the bony spines on the fins.

Some very recent fossil finds in Scotland and in Montana give us an idea of how varied some of the early sharks were. In the seas of the early Carboniferous period there were some amazing sharks with strange spines on their heads.

One of these strange sharks had a bony spine at the back of its head that was shaped like a shaving brush. It was covered with small teeth, and there were also teeth on the forehead. Another one, *Falcatus*, had a long bony spine that pointed forward over its head. One suggestion is that these spines may have been used to scare away bigger sharks.

Some of the most gigantic of the sharks were much bigger than the ones we know today. *Carcharodon*, which lived 30 million years ago, was probably up to 65 feet long. Its teeth were up to 6 inches long, and it could have swallowed a human being in one gulp.

WEIRD SHARKS

There were some very strange-looking sharks in the seas of the Carboniferous. Some of them had strange, elaborate spines on top of their heads. No one knows what these were used for. Some of these sharks were only discovered in 1986.

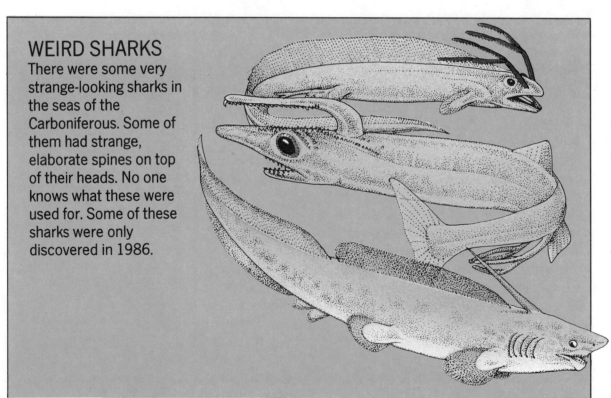

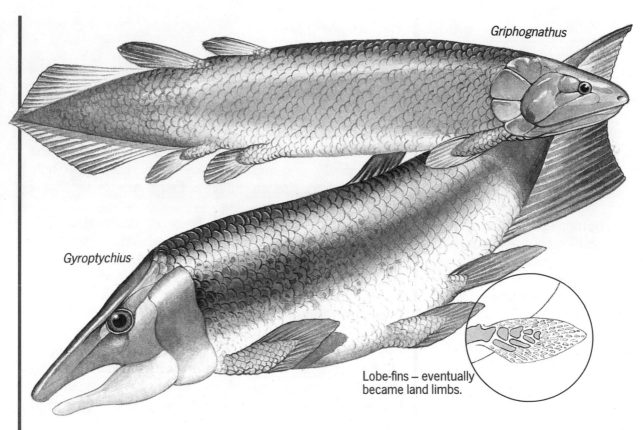

Griphognathus

Gyroptychius

Lobe-fins – eventually
became land limbs.

The bony fish

The first fish with a skeleton made of bone appeared in
the Devonian. These marked the beginning of the most
important of the fish groups. Long after all of the armored
and spiny fish of the Devonian and Carboniferous had
disappeared, the seas of the world were dominated by
bony fish, as they are today.

Most of the bony fish of the Devonian were **lobe-
finned** fish — that is, the fins had a fleshy central area,
or lobe. These were very different from the fins of most
modern fish, which have no fleshy lobe at all.

Lobe-fins and living fossils

Two typical Devonian lobe-fins were *Griphognathus* and
Gyroptychius. Unlike the ostracoderms and placoderms,
they did not have heavily armored heads. Their bodies
were covered by heavy scales, but both fish could
probably have bent their bodies easily to help them swim
well. Fossils of these lobe-finned fish were collected in
Devonian rocks that were laid down on the bottom of a
great warm-water lake that once covered the north of
Scotland. One of the famous early collectors was a man
called Hugh Miller, who discovered many new species.

Griphognathus was an early **lung fish**. Lung fish have
lungs just like human beings, which means that they can
breathe air. They can also breathe underwater through
gills, as normal fish do. Their lungs help them to survive

*Above: two examples of
lobe-finned fish.*
*Below: Hugh Miller (1802-
1856), was a stonemason in
Cromarty, Scotland. He
became a famous collector
of fossil fish.*

34

in warm countries where lakes occasionally dry out. Lung fish were very common in Devonian times, and there are still three species left in tropical waters. These modern forms are often called living fossils because they seem to be survivors from a world that existed 400 million years ago.

Gyroptychius was a different type of lobe-finned fish. It lurked in shallow waters, using its stout fins to hold its body clear of the bottom. It also had lungs for breathing air. It seems likely that the first animals to crawl onto the land arose from a fish like *Gyroptychius*. Some close relatives of *Gyroptychius*, called **coelacanths**, lived on into the age of the dinosaurs.

For many years it was thought that coelacanths had died out long ago. However, a very exciting discovery was made in 1938. Off the coast of South Africa, some fishermen caught a strange blue-colored fish. It was very large, being as much as 6 feet long. They took it back to a museum, where a scientist called Dr. J.L.B. Smith eventually realized that he had a specimen of a modern coelacanth. He offered a reward for more specimens, and eventually some more were caught. This coelacanth is another example of a living fossil.

The living coelacanth, first caught in 1938. This rare fish lives in deep waters in the Indian Ocean off the coast of Africa.

THE FISH
The Devonian period saw the disappearance of the early armored fish and the rise of the cartilaginous and bony fish. Most of the fish we see today are ray-finned bony fish. Lobe-finned bony fish are much rarer.

Key to fish evolution:
1 Ostracoderms
2 Placoderms
3 Cartilaginous fish
4 Bony fish
5 Lobe-finned bony fish
6 Lampreys
7 Sharks
8 Rays
9 Ray-finned bony fish
10 Lungfish
11 Coelacanth
12 To amphibians

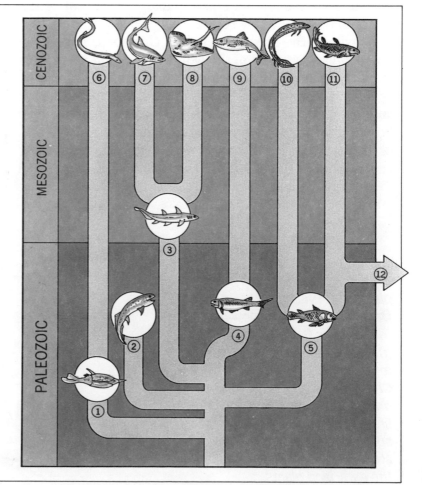

3. Life Moves onto Land

Conquering the land

The early stages in the history of life all took place in the sea. There was no life on land at all for many thousands of millions of years. Eventually, near the end of the Silurian period some plants and small animals moved out of the water and onto the shores.

Fossils of the simple land plant *Cooksonia* have been found in various parts of the world. *Cooksonia* was a very simple small plant that grew in marshy areas. It had many problems to overcome. First of all, it had to be able to support itself. In water, plants such as seaweeds simply float, but on land, they need stiff stems. It had no leaves or flowers, but it had to develop roots to take in water and food from the soil. Sea plants can take in water and food through their leaves.

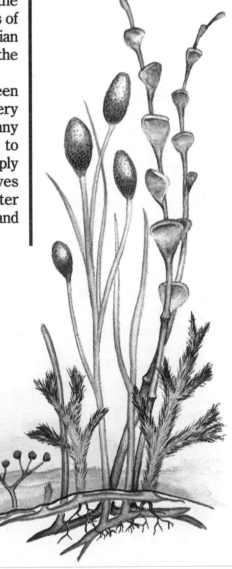

On the right are some of the plants that lived in early Devonian times. We know of these plants from fossils that were found in a rock formation called Rhynie Chert, in Scotland. This was once a peat bog, where the first insects, mites, and spiders lived among the stems and seed cases of the early land plants.

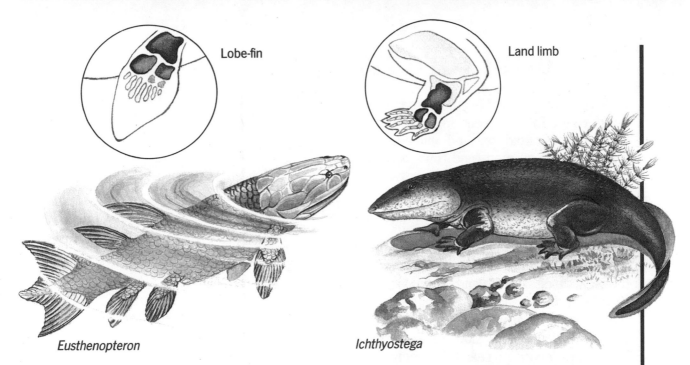

Lobe-fin

Land limb

Eusthenopteron

Ichthyostega

Crawling onto land

By the end of the Devonian there were many more plants and small animals on land. The lobe-finned fish, which could breathe underwater like normal fish as well as in the air, hunted for insects around the edge of the water. These lobe-finned fish had strong, fleshy fins that they used to drag themselves through shallow water, or even over the land for short distances — just like living mudskipper fish. The lobe-fins were well suited to life in the hot Devonian climate. Their ponds often dried up in the heat, and they would have died if they could not have staggered over land to find another pond.

Fins and legs

Some of the lobe-fins gradually became better and better at breathing air, while their fleshy fins became stronger. Over millions of years, they evolved to hold their bodies up, and their fins turned into sturdy legs. The first backboned animals with true legs are known from the late Devonian period — these are the first **amphibians**. Many fossils of the early amphibian *Ichthyostega* have been found in Greenland and footprints have been found in many other parts of the world.

Scientists have compared the bones in the fin of a lobe-finned fish with the bones in the arm of an early amphibian. It turns out that many lobe-finned fish, especially those like *Gyroptychius* or its relative *Eusthenopteron*, already had the same bones in their lobe-fins as the early amphibians had in their arms and hands. Indeed, we still have these same bones — one in the upper arm, two in the lower arm, and five fingers. In other words, our arm and hand are not all that different from the lobe-fin of a Devonian fish!

Near the end of the Devonian, Eusthenopteron crawled out of the water to feed on the many plants and insects that now lived on land. Its lobe-fin did not have to change much to become the leg of the amphibian Ichthyostega, and the same bones can be seen in both.

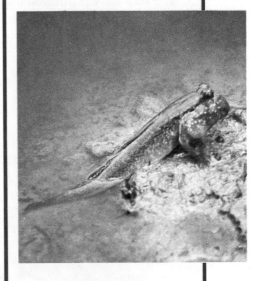

The little mudskipper is a bony fish that spends much of its time out of water. Is this how the first fish crawled out of the sea, millions of years ago?

The coal forests

Life on land really became important during the Carboniferous. In the great forests, the tall trees buzzed with insects, spiders, and millipedes. The amphibians also became common, and toward the end of this period the first reptiles made their appearance.

Trees and coal

The "trees" of the Carboniferous forests were very different from those of today. Some of these early plants belonged to groups that have since died out, such as club mosses, tree ferns, and seed ferns. The club moss *Lepidodendron* reached a height of 150 feet, while the tree fern *Psaronius* looked rather like a palm tree. Others were giant versions of their living relatives — the horsetail *Calamites* reached a height of 52 feet, while living horsetails are usually less than 2 feet tall.

The Carboniferous forests of Europe and North America were hot, damp places, with almost tropical climates. There were low ferns and small bushes around the ponds and rivers, and the trees stood farther back. Most of them had massive tree trunks, and the leaves were usually long branching fronds, like the leaves of living ferns.

As time went by, these forests built up thick layers of leaves and dead timber on the forest floor and in the water. The leaves and wood soon turned into soft peat that eventually hardened into coal. Nearly all the coal that is mined in the world today was formed from the Carboniferous coal swamp forests.

An old engraving showing fossilized tree trunks in a coal seam. Coal miners knew about the remains of these Carboniferous trees many centuries ago, long before scientists fully understood what kinds of plants they were.

The Carboniferous coal forests were full of life. In the litter of leaves on the ground, giant millipedes up to 6 feet long crept about seeking food, while spiders wove their webs in the trees in order to trap flying insects.

Giant dragonflies the size of seagulls flew in and out of the waterside trees. Other insects, such as cockroaches and grasshoppers, ran around on plant stems. Some of them had long piercing beaks that they used to puncture the stems to suck sap. Other insects ate seeds or leaves. Fossils of Carboniferous plants often show signs of their prehistoric nibblings!

A coal swamp forest scene showing horsetails and ferns around the water's edge. The trees Lepidodendron *and* Calamites *grow in the distance. The huge dragonfly* Meganeura *flies above the forest floor, where the giant millipede* Arthropleura *and early centipedes and cockroaches creep around.*

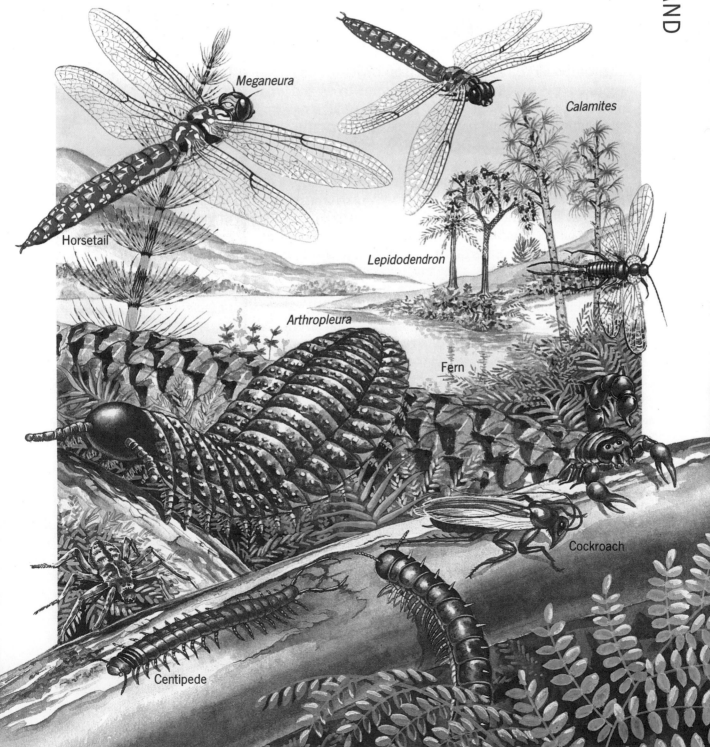

Meganeura

Calamites

Horsetail

Lepidodendron

Arthropleura

Fern

Cockroach

Centipede

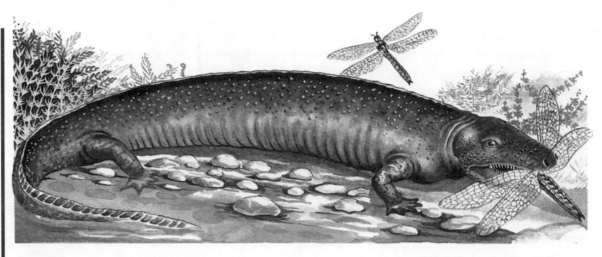

Life on land

The Carboniferous amphibians found all the food they wanted in the coal swamps, with their tall trees and large insects. Just like their living relatives, the frogs and salamanders, they had to live very close to water in order to stop their skins from drying out. Their eggs were also laid in water for the same reason.

Most of the Carboniferous amphibians were heavily built animals like *Eogyrinus*. This **labyrinthodont** had a broad flat head and many small teeth that were used to capture insects and fish. Baby amphibians have also been found in the Carboniferous rocks of some parts of the world. One example is a small animal called *Branchiosaurus* that had feathery gills for breathing under water, just as tadpoles have today.

Some of the later amphibians moved away from the water. In the Permian period, a number of large amphibians such as *Eryops* had come to live in desertlike conditions. They must have had thicker, tougher skins to

Fossils of Eogyrinus, *a Carboniferous amphibian, have been found in England. Eogyrinus* was 13 feet long. *It probably lived rather like a crocodile, feeding on fish and waterside animals.*

The small amphibian Branchiosaurus *had feathery gills on the side of its neck, which show that it breathed underwater. It might have been a young tadpolelike animal, though some scientists suggest that it might be a grown animal that had evolved to live underwater all of the time.*

keep the water in. However, they probably still had to return to the water to lay their eggs. These large land-living amphibians did not survive long in the Permian.

Some other groups of Carboniferous amphibians evolved back toward life in the water. Many of these animals, called **lepospondyls**, probably lived in the water most of the time. Some were as small as living newts or salamanders. Others even lost their legs and lived like water snakes, swimming by twisting the body from side to side.

The most remarkable of the water-living lepospondyls of the Carboniferous was *Diplocaulus*. It had a head shaped like a boomerang, with a large "horn" sticking out on either side. The head was flat, and the horns were actually firmly attached to the head since they were part of the skull. It is very hard to guess what this strange creature did with its bizzare head. One idea is that it allowed *Diplocaulus* to open its mouth wide very quickly. *Diplocaulus* might have hunted by creeping up on a small fish, and then opening its mouth so quickly that the fish was sucked in before it knew what had happened.

Eryops was a Permian amphibian that has been found in Texas. It lived well away from the water in dry, desertlike conditions. It was a strongly built animal, about 5 feet long, and it may have fed on smaller amphibians and on insects.

The strange amphibian Diplocaulus lived in the water most of the time. Its strange "horns" may have been used in defense, to make it difficult for larger amphibians to eat it.

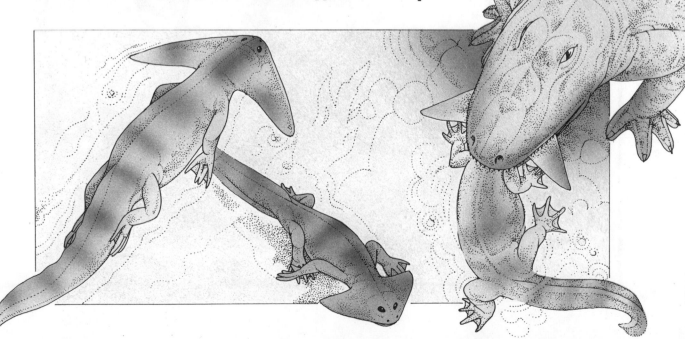

On dry land

The Carboniferous period is often called the Age of Amphibians, because of the sturdy labyrinthodonts and the smaller lepospondyls that lived in the coal swamp forests. By Permian times, labyrinthodonts like *Eryops* lived in dry conditions, and the lepospondyls were more like lizards.

In the Permian, another group of amphibians took the move to life on dry land a step further. *Diadectes* and *Seymouria* seem to have been almost completely adapted to life away from the water. *Diadectes* was heavily built and it had more powerful legs than many of the earlier amphibians. This suggests that it moved more quickly on land. It was also very different from the earlier amphibians in another way. Instead of having sharp little teeth for biting fish or insects, *Diadectes* had blunt peglike teeth. This shows that it ate leaves and the roots of plants — it seems to have been the first plant-eating amphibian to have evolved.

Seymouria and *Diadectes* may have laid their eggs on land. Some very ancient fossil eggs have been found in Texas, which may have been laid by *Seymouria*. They have a hard egg shell, just like a hen's egg, and this shows that they were not laid in water. Normally, the eggs of amphibians do not have a shell. Frog spawn is soft and jellylike, and we assume that the eggs of typical Carboniferous amphibians were the same.

Many of the early amphibians had died out by the end of the Permian period, although a few labyrinthodonts

Diadectes and Seymouria *lived in Permian times. These amphibians may have lived fully on dry land, and many scientists have even argued that they were not really amphibians at all.*

Diadectes

Seymouria

THE AMPHIBIANS

The stocky labyrinthodonts and the smaller lepospondyls lived in Paleozoic times. The modern amphibians (frogs, salamanders, and the **apodans**) appeared in the Mesozoic. They are so unlike the amphibians that came before them that their origin is a mystery.

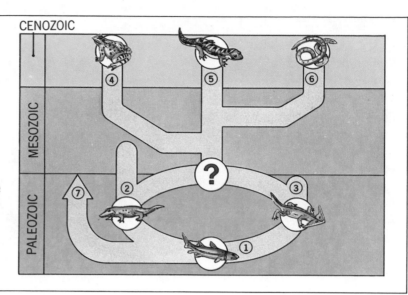

lived on into the age of the dinosaurs. The modern types of amphibians — frogs, newts, and salamanders — appeared during this time. The oldest known frog skeleton comes from the early Triassic. It has a round-fronted skull, short arms, very long legs, and a short fat body. The great mystery is where the frogs and salamanders came from. No one knows the answer to this, since these modern forms are so different from the labyrinthodonts and lepospondyls.

Key to amphibian evolution:
1 Lobe-finned fish
2 Labyrinthodonts
3 Lepospondyls
4 Frogs and toads
5 Newts and salamanders
6 Apodans
7 To reptiles

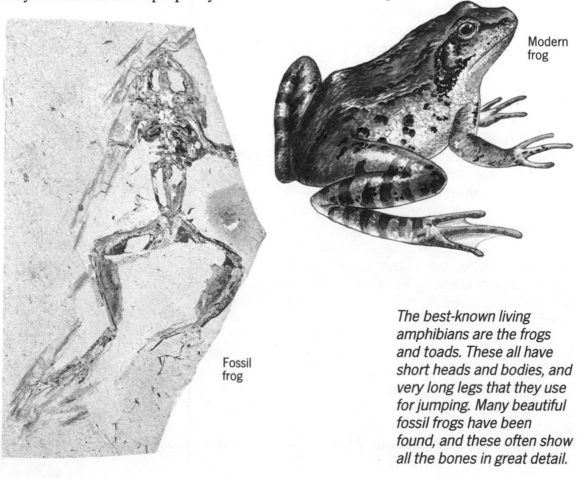

Fossil frog

Modern frog

The best-known living amphibians are the frogs and toads. These all have short heads and bodies, and very long legs that they use for jumping. Many beautiful fossil frogs have been found, and these often show all the bones in great detail.

43

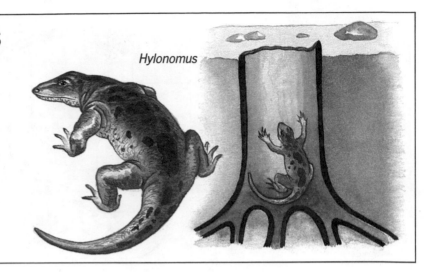

FOSSIL SURVIVORS

Early reptiles such as *Hylonomus* darted among the stumps of fallen trees in search of insects and snails. If they fell into an old hollow tree stump that was full of water, their drowned bodies were preserved as fossils inside the fossil tree.

Hylonomus

The rise of the reptiles

The lush coal swamp forests of the Carboniferous gradually disappeared in the Permian period, and North America and Europe became drier. Some of the primitive amphibians were able to live in these conditions but others died out. During these changing times, a major new group of land animals came on the scene that were to dominate the earth for the next 250 million years. These were the **reptiles**.

The first reptiles

Like the reptiles we know today, such as lizards, snakes, and turtles, these early reptiles could lay their eggs away from the water. Unlike those of the amphibians, the eggs had a tough outer skin that stopped them from drying out. The first reptiles probably evolved from relatives of amphibians like *Diadectes* and *Seymouria*. The earliest to be found was *Hylonomus*, a small lizardlike animal from the Carboniferous period that fed on insects and spiders.

By Permian times, a whole new range of reptiles had come on the scene. The most important were the **mammallike reptiles**.

One special group of mammallike reptiles were the **sail-backs**, which lived in the Lower Permian of North America and Europe. Most had tall bony spines along their backs that were covered in skin. This may have been used as a kind of radiator to control their body temperature. When the reptile was cold, it would turn sideways to the sun so that the blood vessels in its "sail" could take in heat. When it got too hot, it would turn its

Sail-backed reptiles like Dimetrodon *and* Edaphosaurus *may have used their sails to control their body temperatures.*

Varanosaurus

REPTILE EGGS

Unlike the amphibians, reptiles lay eggs with a hard tough outer shell that protects the baby inside and stops it from drying out. The amphibian egg has no shell (like frog spawn) and it has to be laid in water to keep it moist.

back to the sun so that the sail could give off heat. Some of the sail-backs, like *Varanosaurus*, did not actually have a sail. It was once thought that sail-backs with sails were male and those without were female, but this cannot be the case as the two types are usually found in rocks of different ages.

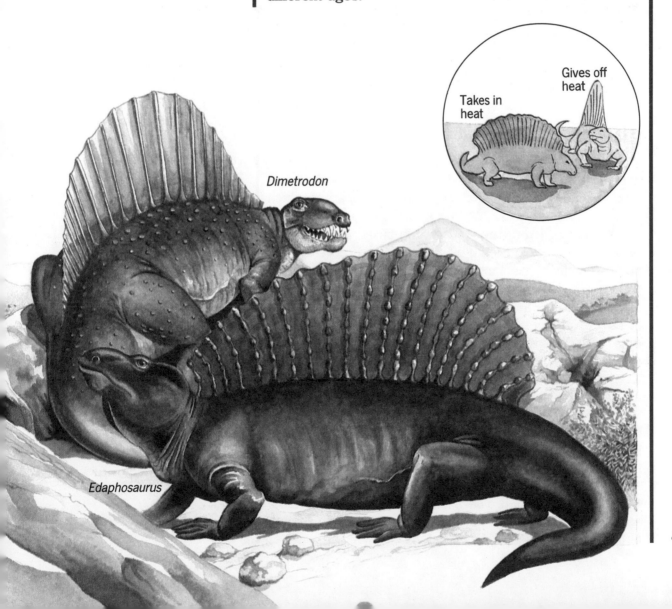

Takes in heat

Gives off heat

Dimetrodon

Edaphosaurus

45

Dicynodon

Scutosaurus

Mammallike reptiles

The mammallike reptiles dominated the land during the late Permian. There were small ones, no larger than a mouse, and giant ones the size of a rhinoceros. These animals lived in landscapes full of primitive bushes and trees. One very common tree was *Glossopteris*, which grew in many parts of the world at this time.

The **gorgonopsians** ("gorgon-faces"), such as *Sauroctonus*, were medium- to large-sized meat-eaters, some of which had fangs. The **dinocephalians** ("terrible heads") included both meat-eaters and plant-eaters like *Moschops*, a strange bulky-looking animal whose arms were longer than its legs. The **dicynodonts** ("two dog-teeth"), such as *Dicynodon*, were very common plant-eaters during the late Permian and the Triassic. They were fat tusked creatures, with a long gut to digest all the rough plant food they ate.

Other land animals of the late Permian included the ugly **pareiasaurs** like *Scutosaurus*. Their knobby heads had lots of small bumps and horns, and their skin may also have been covered in warts. The pareiasaurs used their small, sawlike teeth to slice up plants. Smaller reptiles of these times included *Youngina* — a primitive lizardlike animal with a long slim body that probably fed on insects and snails.

The fierce-looking Moschops *and* Scutosaurus *were actually peaceful plant-eaters that used their sharp teeth for slicing up vegetation. Protected by their tough, bone-studded hides, they lived alongside fierce meat-eaters like* Sauroctonus — *here seen in pursuit of the lizardlike* Youngina.

Glossopteris

Moschops

Sauroctonus

Youngina

Dying in droves

At the end of the Permian, a major catastrophe occurred. For some unknown reason, more than half of all the species of plants and animals died out at the same time. The late Permian seas and lands were suddenly emptied of life. A few species of mammallike reptiles lived on, but the gorgonopsians, dinocephalians, and pareiasaurs were completely wiped out.

No one knows what caused the mass extinction of the late Permian, but it is thought that it may have been the result of major changes in sea level and climates.

THE GREAT DYING

A huge variety of reptiles crawled over the late Permian landscape. Suddenly, at the end of the Permian, most of these were mysteriously wiped out. Only a few species of plant-eaters and meat-eaters survived. The world after this event must have seemed strangely empty.

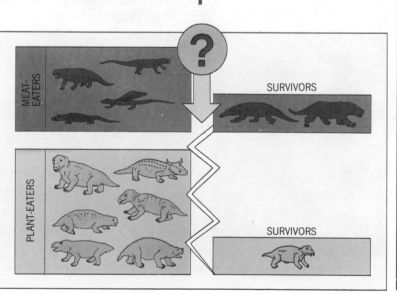

MEAT-EATERS

SURVIVORS

PLANT-EATERS

SURVIVORS

47

The ruling reptiles

The mammallike reptiles never fully recovered from the shock of the great extinction at the end of the Permian. One of the commonest of those that survived was a medium-sized dicynodont called *Lystrosaurus*.

Lystrosaurus fed on plants in and around lakes, where it was preyed on by **cynodonts** like *Cynognathus*. *Cynognathus* was a mammallike reptile that had sharp teeth for biting, and it may even have been covered in hair just like a modern dog. How can scientists guess that *Cynognathus* had hair, since hair is not easily fossilized?

The skull of *Cynognathus* shows small pits on the snout that are exactly the same as those on a dog. These pits are for the small nerves that are connected to the whiskers that a dog uses to feel its way around. If *Cynognathus* had whiskers, it must also have had hair on other parts of its body. This suggests that cynodonts may have been **warm-blooded**, just like mammals today.

 *Lystrosaurus*

By the beginning of the Triassic, all the continents had drifted together to form a single super-continent. This made it possible for animals like Lystrosaurus *to spread all over the world.*

An early Triassic scene in southern Africa. Two bulky Lystrosaurus *feed on soft water plants, while the meat-eating cynodonts* Cynognathus *feed on a* Lystrosaurus *that they have just killed.*

Lystrosaurus

Cynognathus

Proterosuchus

Shansisuchus

The mammallike reptiles were not to rule the earth for much longer. A new group of meat-eating animals was waiting to take over in this early Triassic world.

The ruling reptiles

These new animals were the **archosaurs** ("ruling reptiles") that had arisen at the end of the Permian. While the mammallike reptiles had branched off in one direction from early reptiles like *Hylonomus*, the archosaurs came from a different line that also led to the lizards and snakes. The Triassic archosaurs are called the **thecodontians**.

Two of the earliest were *Proterosuchus* and *Shansisuchus*. *Proterosuchus* was shaped rather like a small crocodile, and probably fed on small animals and fish. *Shansisuchus* was taller than *Proterosuchus*, and it could probably have run very fast. It was the biggest animal of its day, and clearly a fearsome meat-eater.

During the Triassic, the thecodontians gave rise to a number of other important lines. These included the ancestors of the crocodiles and the pterosaurs. Most importantly, it led to the animals that dominated the earth for so many millions of years — the dinosaurs.

The crocodilelike Proterosuchus *had short legs and a long, flat-sided tail that may have been used for swimming. Its jaw was lined with sharp teeth.* Shansisuchus *was a larger animal with a massive head and powerful jaws.*

49

Staurikosaurus

Scaphonyx

Enter the dinosaurs

A rather odd group of reptiles called the **rhynchosaurs** came on the scene in the middle of the Triassic. They had long hooked beaks that they probably used to rake up stems and roots of plants. They also had powerful jaws and remarkable sets of teeth that allowed them to slice through very tough plants as if with a strong pair of scissors. These heavily built animals became very common in nearly all parts of the world. They seem to have taken over as the main plant-eaters everywhere, after the death of most of the mammallike reptiles. However, the rhynchosaurs were around for only a very short time, and they disappeared long before the Triassic was over.

At the same time as the last rhynchosaurs were contentedly munching their way through the under-growth, a small archosaur called *Staurikosaurus* was running about. *Staurikosaurus* is known from fossils found in Brazil. It was a fairly small, lightly built animal that stood and ran on its hind legs only. This was one of the first dinosaurs.

If you had gone back to these times, you would not have found the dinosaurs particularly impressive. They were small, and very rare. However, another great extinction was soon to take place. The rhynchosaurs and

A late Triassic scene in South America, showing the bulky rhynchosaurs Scaphonyx *and the early dinosaur* Staurikosaurus.

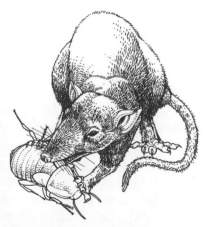

Morganucodon, one of the first mammals, has been found in Triassic rocks in Wales and China.

50

many of the mammallike reptiles and thecodontians disappeared completely. The early rare dinosaurs survived, and soon became far more common. They also became much larger, until the days when giants like *Apatosaurus* walked the earth.

The mammals

Some of the mammallike reptiles, such as the doglike *Cynognathus*, were probably warm-blooded. The first true mammals evolved from these mammallike reptiles in the late Triassic. All of the hairy animals that we know today are mammals — the cats, dogs, horses, bats, rabbits, and humans.

The first mammals were quite small creatures, such as the shrewlike *Morganucodon*. They had small sharp teeth, and probably fed on insects and worms. For millions of years, these little animals scuttled about past the feet of the giant dinosaurs. Their importance was not to come until later on, when the age of the dinosaurs came to a sudden and mysterious end.

THE REPTILES

Reptiles no longer rule the earth, as they did millions of years ago. However, they did give rise to today's most important animal group, the mammals.

Key to reptile evolution:
1 Early amphibians
2 Archosaurs
3 Sail-backs
4 Early dinosaurs
5 Mammallike reptiles
6 Plesiosaurs
7 Pterosaurs
8 Lizard-hipped dinosaurs
9 *Archaeopteryx*
10 Bird-hipped dinosaurs
11 Ichthyosaurs
12 Turtles
13 Birds
14 Crocodiles
15 Lizards
16 Snakes
17 Mammals

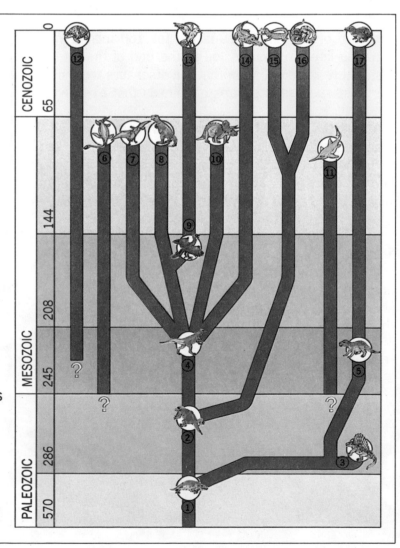

51

4. When the Dinosaurs Ruled

The world of the dinosaurs

The rule of the dinosaurs lasted for 160 million years, from the late Triassic period to the end of the Cretaceous. There is no question that the dinosaurs were one of the most successful groups of animals that ever lived.

At the time when the dinosaurs first appeared, all the continents of the earth were joined together in one single land mass. This meant that animals could wander freely all over the world. Today, the same species of dinosaur may be found as far apart as Africa and the United States.

Giant dinosaurs like Brachiosaurus *stood as tall as a three-story building and as long as five buses parked end to end. However, other dinosaurs were only the size of a chicken.*

Triceratops

Compsognathus

WHY SO BIG?
Brachiosaurus was one of the largest dinosaurs, standing 40 feet high. Its great bulk would have helped it to keep its body temperature even, since the skin area (through which heat is lost or taken in) was relatively small in proportion to the rest of its body.

Brachiosaurus

The weather was also warmer and less changeable everywhere. Today there is a big difference between the hot lands at the equator and the icy North and South Poles. But paleontologists have found skeletons of dinosaurs inside the Arctic Circle, so the weather must have been quite mild at that time even as far north as that.

On land, there were reptiles similar to the crocodiles, lizards, and turtles that are around today. The mammals that lived at this time were mostly little insect-eaters that looked like shrews and rats. Most of the trees were primitive ferns and horsetails. There were some conifers like present-day redwoods and monkey puzzle trees. In the skies, flying reptiles grew up to the size of a small glider. The seas were also dominated by the reptiles. These included the plesiosaurs and the dolphinlike ichthyosaurs.

Anatosaurus

Tyrannosaurus

Stegosaurus

Deinonychus

Ornitholestes

The first dinosaurs

The first dinosaurs lived 225 million years ago in the late Triassic. One of the earliest was found in Brazil. *Staurikosaurus* was a small, 6½-foot long animal that stood upright and ran about on its hind legs. Its arms were shorter than its legs, and were probably used to pick up food. The dinosaurs came from a group of thecodontians that had their legs right underneath the body. Most of the mammallike reptiles, rhynchosaurs, and thecodontians of the Permian and Triassic had their legs sticking out sideways, in what is called the *sprawling* position. Dinosaurs held their legs in the *upright* position, which meant they could run much faster.

Dinosaurs were still rather rare in these early times in Brazil. Much more common were the rhynchosaurs and the mammallike reptiles. However, only one or two million years later, the dinosaurs were masters of the earth. How did this happen?

The rise of the dinosaurs

There was another great mass extinction during the late Triassic. This wiped out most of the mammallike reptiles and thecodontians, and all of the rhynchosaurs. Small dinosaurs like *Staurikosaurus* survived, and soon spread out all over the world.

Skeletons of the early dinosaur *Coelophysis* have been found in many parts of North America. *Coelophysis* was

Staurikosaurus, *one of the earliest dinosaurs, is known from only one or two incomplete skeletons. It had sharp meat-eating teeth, and it probably fed on small mammallike reptiles.*

Coelophysis, *an early dinosaur from North America, had long legs and a very long neck and tail. It was a meat-eater, and might even have been a cannibal. Some fossils show tiny skeletons of baby* Coelophysis *inside it that may have just been eaten.*

Plateosaurus

Pterosaur

Crocodile

Procompsognathus

about 10 feet long, and it had a very slender body. It would have been able to run fast in order to chase its prey. In 1947, a hundred or more skeletons of *Coelophysis* were found at Ghost Ranch in New Mexico. These included young and old animals, and it seems that a whole herd of them must have become stuck in a boggy area.

In southwest Germany, several dozen skeletons of the dinosaur *Plateosaurus* have been dug up over the past 150 years. *Plateosaurus* was a very different kind of dinosaur from *Staurikosaurus* and *Coelophysis*. It was much larger, being up to 26 feet long, and it was probably a plant-eater. *Plateosaurus* probably walked on all fours, although it could still stand up on its hind legs. It was an ancestor of the later giant plant-eating dinosaurs, like *Apatosaurus*.

Plateosaurus lived with other dinosaurs such as the smaller meat-eating *Procompsognathus*, which fed on small lizards and frogs. There were also early crocodiles, mammals, and some of the first pterosaurs that flew among the branches of the trees.

A scene from southwestern Germany in late Triassic times. The large plant-eater Plateosaurus *feeds in the background, while the smaller meat-eating* Procompsognathus *runs past. There are also early crocodiles and pterosaurs.*

PLATEOSAURUS

Plateosaurus had a long narrow snout. Its jaws were lined with small peg-like teeth that could only have been used for eating plants.
Plateosaurus had large strong hands, and the thumb had a very large claw that may have been used for raking leaves together or for dragging branches down to its mouth.

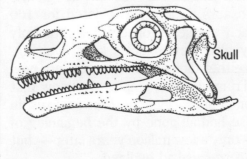

Skull

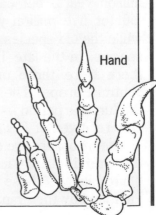

Hand

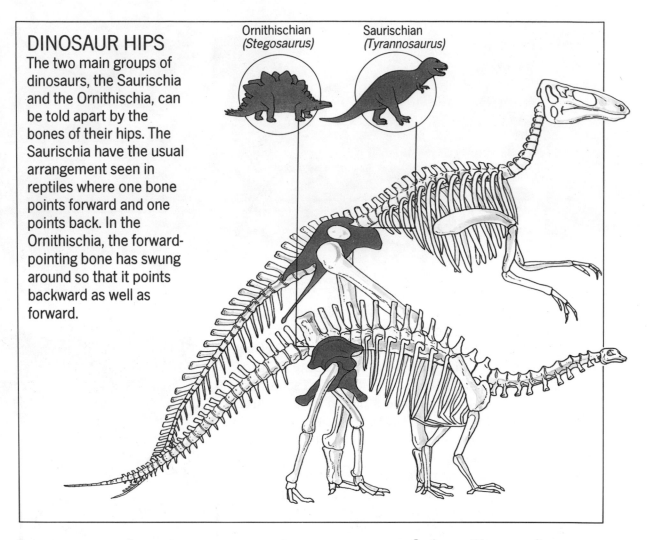

DINOSAUR HIPS

The two main groups of dinosaurs, the Saurischia and the Ornithischia, can be told apart by the bones of their hips. The Saurischia have the usual arrangement seen in reptiles where one bone points forward and one points back. In the Ornithischia, the forward-pointing bone has swung around so that it points backward as well as forward.

Ornithischian (*Stegosaurus*)

Saurischian (*Tyrannosaurus*)

Lizard-hips and bird-hips

There were at least 500 species of dinosaurs, and there are probably many more yet to be discovered. Every year, scientists discover new dinosaurs all over the world, so that the total number keeps getting bigger. Of course, all 500 species of dinosaurs did not live at the same time. The dinosaurs as a whole existed for 160 million years, but each species probably lived for only four or five million years. New species kept evolving, while the old species either died out or changed into new species. In the late Triassic, for example, we know that there were three or four species of *Plateosaurus* in central Europe. These had all gone by the beginning of the Jurassic period — only a few million years later — but new relatives of *Plateosaurus* had evolved.

The dinosaurs are divided into two main groups, called the **Saurischia** ("lizard-hips") and the **Ornithischia** ("bird-hips"). These two big groups of dinosaurs are identified by their hip regions, as their names suggest. In

An exciting new dinosaur was discovered in 1983 by William Walker in an early Cretaceous clay pit in Surrey, England. In 1986 it was named Baryonyx walkeri.

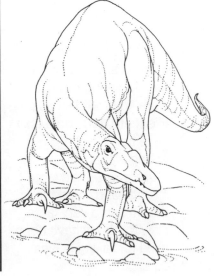

the hip region of the skeleton in reptiles there are three separate bones. The two lower bones point in different directions in the two dinosaur groups, as shown in the picture on the opposite page.

Deadly claws and spiny armor

Saurischian dinosaurs appeared in the late Triassic. The earliest types were small meat-eaters like *Coelophysis,* but new groups evolved in the Jurassic and Cretaceous. These included ferocious **carnosaurs** like *Megalosaurus* and *Tyrannosaurus,* the slender ostrich dinosaur *Struthiomimus,* and the deadly **deinonychosaurs,** which had huge claws on their feet. The first plant-eating saurischians could walk on all fours or on their hind legs, but these early **prosauropods**, like *Plateosaurus,* became much larger in the Jurassic. They evolved into **sauropods**, such as *Apatosaurus,* which probably always walked on all fours.

It is not certain when the ornithischian dinosaurs first came on the scene. The first ones were quite small, and walked on their hind limbs. These **ornithopods** became larger during the Jurassic and Cretaceous, and included the duckbilled dinosaurs called **hadrosaurs**. The ornithopods also gave rise to the strange-looking armored dinosaurs. The **stegosaurs** had spines and plates on their backs, the **ankylosaurs** had bony plates set in their skin, and the **ceratopsians** had sharp horns on their snouts and on the tops of their heads. These armored dinosaurs were all plant-eaters.

Key to dinosaur evolution:
1. Coelurosaurs
2. Deinonychosaurs
3. Ornithomimosaurs
4. Carnosaurs
5. Prosauropods
6. Sauropods
7. Ornithopods
8. Stegosaurs
9. Ankylosaurs
10. Ceratopsians

The Jurassic scene

Some of the best-known dinosaurs lived during Jurassic times. Climates were warm, and much of the earth was covered with lush forests of conifers, seed ferns, and cycads. By the late Jurassic, most of the major dinosaur groups had come onto the scene. Some of the richest dinosaur beds of this age have been found in the western United States.

Over a hundred years ago, the great American bone hunters Othniel Marsh and Edward Cope started to find large dinosaur skeletons in Utah and Colorado. Most of these fossil finds came from late Jurassic rocks that had been laid down in a huge coastal area of river channels and swamps that lay just to the east of the Rocky Mountains. These rocks have been termed the Morrison Formation.

Dinosaurs of the Morrison Formation in the late Jurassic. The plated Stegosaurus *munches on leaves, while the meat-eating* Allosaurus *looks on hungrily. In the background is the giant sauropod* Brachiosaurus.

Brachiosaurus

Allosaurus

Stegosaurus

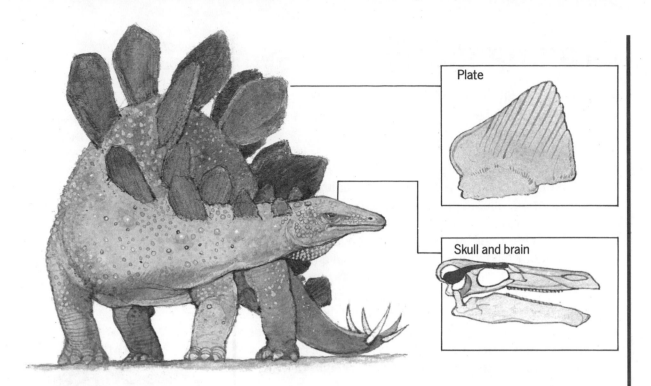

Plate

Skull and brain

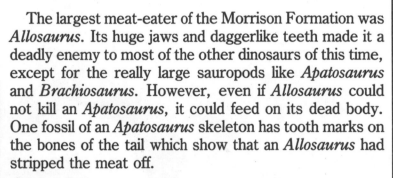

Pterosaur

Stegosaurus had a number of large diamond-shaped plates on its back. It may have absorbed or lost heat through the plates, just as the sail-backed reptiles did in the Permian. Stegosaurus is often said to be the stupidest of the dinosaurs, as its tiny brain was the size of a walnut.

The largest meat-eater of the Morrison Formation was *Allosaurus*. Its huge jaws and daggerlike teeth made it a deadly enemy to most of the other dinosaurs of this time, except for the really large sauropods like *Apatosaurus* and *Brachiosaurus*. However, even if *Allosaurus* could not kill an *Apatosaurus*, it could feed on its dead body. One fossil of an *Apatosaurus* skeleton has tooth marks on the bones of the tail which show that an *Allosaurus* had stripped the meat off.

Plates for protection

One of the best-known dinosaurs of the Morrison Formation is *Stegosaurus*, the plated dinosaur. *Stegosaurus* was about 30 feet long, and it walked on all fours. Unusually, its front legs were very short compared to the hind legs, and this suggests that its ancestors had once walked upright. This means that *Stegosaurus* held its head quite close to the ground.

Stegosaurus had about 24 plates along its back, and four spines on its tail. The plates were arranged in two rows, but not exactly opposite each other. They were fixed deep into the skin, but they were not part of the normal bony skeleton. The plates probably stood upright, although it has been suggested that they might have stuck out sideways. The spines on the tail were probably used for defense. *Stegosaurus* could swing its tail from side to side with great force to scare away any meat-eater that tried to attack. The purpose of the plates on the back is not so clear. They might have been used for defense, or, as with the sail-back reptiles, they might have helped in controlling its body temperature.

59

Grazing giants

Food was readily available for the large plant-eating sauropods of the late Jurassic, and they grew to be the largest land animals of all time.

   Brachiosaurus was the biggest well-known sauropod. When this giant reared its head right up, it could have looked over the roof of a three-story building. An even larger sauropod, nicknamed *Supersaurus*, has not been properly named yet, as only part of the skeleton has been discovered. One bone of the neck was over 5 feet long, and its shoulder blade was much longer than a man. It has been estimated that *Supersaurus* was 100 feet long and 50 feet high. Bones of an even bigger animal, known as *Ultrasaurus*, were found in 1979. It might have been up to 115 feet long and 100-140 tons in weight. These figures are only guesses, but if they are correct then these dinosaurs were up to 20 times the weight of a large elephant!

A herd of the slender sauropod Barosaurus. Fossils of Barosaurus *have been found as far apart as the United States and East Africa. This helps to prove that the huge dinosaur could travel between the two areas — in other words, that the continents were joined together at this time.*

The three largest dinosaurs, all known from the Morrison Formation of the United States. Brachiosaurus *is the biggest well-known dinosaur, while the bones that have been found belonging to* Supersaurus *and* Ultrasaurus *suggest that they were almost certainly larger.*

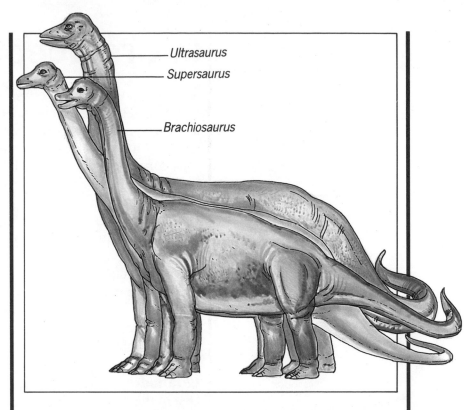

Ultrasaurus
Supersaurus
Brachiosaurus

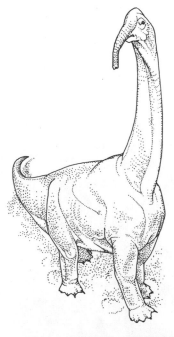

It was once thought that sauropods had trunks like elephants, because their nostrils were high up on their faces. The trunk could have been used to gather plant food. However, very few scientists accept this idea now.

How could these giants have eaten enough to stay alive? They all had tiny heads with small mouths and very long necks. Could they have chewed up enough food and swallowed it fast enough to keep going? The sauropods were all plant-eaters. Their blunt peglike teeth were very weak, and they must have torn up mouthfuls of leaves and stems and swallowed them nearly whole since they could not chew their food.

On land, or afloat

At one time, scientists thought that the giant sauropods spent most of their time standing in deep lakes. It seemed impossible that they could have supported their own weight on land, but water would have allowed them to float. However, a tall dinosaur like *Brachiosaurus* could not have sucked enough air down into its lungs to breathe if it was standing in deep water.

Other scientists then suggested that the sauropods lived like giant giraffes, using their long necks to browse for leaves at the tops of the highest trees. The problem with this idea is that their hearts were not strong enough to pump the blood all the way up to their brains. The large sauropods like *Brachiosaurus* and *Barosaurus* might have been able to lift their heads high into the trees to snatch some leaves, but they probably lowered their necks quite quickly to swallow them. It seems likely that the sauropods walked around in shallow lakes and on the land. They probably fed on soft plants around the water's edge and also stripped the occasional leaf from high in the lakeside trees.

In Cretaceous times

The Cretaceous was the last age of the dinosaurs. Many new species came on the scene during this time, as well as more modern-looking plants and animals. The early Cretaceous dinosaurs are best known from the Wealden rock formations of the south of England.

Nearly all the giant sauropods of the Jurassic had now died out, and the main plant-eaters were the ornithopods. One of the commonest of these was *Hypsilophodon*, a small active animal about 6½ feet long. *Hypsilophodon* had short arms with strong hands that could be used to pick up bundles of leaves. It had long powerful legs, and it could have run very fast, holding its tail out straight behind for balance. It was once thought that *Hypsilophodon* perched up on the branches of trees, but its feet could not have held onto the branches.

Iguanodon — historic dinosaur

One of the most famous Wealden dinosaurs is *Iguanodon*. Dozens of skeletons of this ornithopod have been

Iguanodon

collected from as far afield as England, Belgium, and North Africa. Some specimens have even been reported from North America.

Iguanodon stood 16 feet high when it stretched up on its hind legs. It is likely that it also walked on all fours, since the arms are very strong. The feet had broad hoof-like nails, and the hand bore a pointed spikelike thumb that might have been used as a weapon.

Like *Hypsilophodon*, *Iguanodon* had no teeth at the front of the mouth — only a bony beak. However, the teeth farther back were very strong and covered with ridges. *Iguanodon* was one of the first animals that was actually able to chew its food instead of swallowing it whole. It probably also had a long strong tongue that it might have used, as a cow does, to grab plants and pull them into its mouth.

In the middle of the Cretaceous period, when the last *Iguanodons* were roaming the earth, they might have come across some amazing new plants — the first flowers. This major plant group, which includes roses and oak trees, cabbages and grasses, was soon to spread all over the world.

The dinosaurs of the Wealden rocks from the south of England. The little ornithopod Hypsilophodon *rummages for food around the water's edge, while* Iguanodon *grazes on the leaves of trees.* Hyleosaurus, *with its thick covering of spines and bony plates, was one of the first armored dinosaurs. There are also some rare sauropods, as well as tortoises and crocodiles, in this warm subtropical landscape.*

Hypsilophodon

Hyleosaurus

The deadliest dinosaurs

The plant-eaters of the Cretaceous lived alongside some of the most ferocious of all the meat-eating dinosaurs. Of these, the carnosaurs were the largest and most deadly. They had long, daggerlike teeth with sharp points and jagged, steak knife edges. Sometimes their plant-eating victim would put up a brave fight, and the carnosaur's teeth would break off in their hides. Fossil teeth are quite common finds because of this. Many of the plant-eaters evolved all kinds of armor and defense, and the meat-eaters had to fight all the harder for their supper.

The tyrant king

One of the deadliest carnosaurs of all was *Tyrannosaurus rex* — the "king tyrant reptile." *Tyrannosaurus* lived in the late Cretaceous of western Canada and the United States, where it was the biggest meat-eater of its day. A fully grown man would have only reached up to *Tyrannosaurus*'s knee, and it would have made only a small snack for this huge dinosaur.

Tyrannosaurus had powerful hind legs that would have allowed it to run quite fast, for short distances at least. However, its arms were tiny and they cannot have been used for much. *Tyrannosaurus* could not even reach its mouth with its hand. Each hand had only two tiny claws. It has been suggested that they might have been used by *Tyrannosaurus* to raise itself from the lying position. If it pushed itself up and flung its great head back, its weight would have shifted to its legs, which could then hoist it up from the ground.

A lightweight killer

Some of the other Cretaceous meat-eaters had huge claws to help to catch their prey. *Deinonychus* had strong grasping fingers on its hands and a huge claw on its hind foot. It was a very lightly built animal that could easily have outrun its prey. It probably fought by slashing out with its great sickle claw and ripping open the belly of its victim. When *Deinonychus* was running, it could fold its claw back so that it did not touch the ground. This also kept it sharp for use in attack.

Terrible hands

A much larger relative of *Deinonychus* is known only from a huge pair of arms, each of which was 8½ feet long. It was named *Deinocheirus*, or "terrible hand." Each hand had only three fingers, and each of these was armed with a powerful claw about 10 inches long — the size of a butcher's heavy chopping knife.

The giant arms of Deinocheirus *were found in the Late Cretaceous rocks of Mongolia. Each arm was much longer than the height of a man. It is hard to work out exactly how big* Deinocheirus *was, but it must have been over 40 feet from snout to tail.*

A Tyrannosaurus rex *tears huge chunks of flesh from the body of a plant-eating dinosaur. No other flesh-eating animal has ever matched this late Cretaceous monster for size and ferociousness.* Spinosaurus *was a strange relative of* Tyrannosaurus. *It had a sail on its back that it might have used to control its body heat, as the sail-backed reptiles did in Permian times.*

Tyrannosaurus

Spinosaurus

Triceratops

Tyrannosaurus

Speed and defense

Struthiomimus would have made a tasty meal for a hungry *Tyrannosaurus* — but only if it stayed still long enough to be caught! This ostrich dinosaur was one of the fastest animals of its day. Running like an ostrich with its body held stiffly, the neck straight up, and the long slender back legs making huge strides, it could probably have overtaken a fast racehorse.

Struthiomimus was a lightly built dinosaur, with a high domed head and big intelligent eyes. Its brain was as quick as its feet, which helped it to raid the nests of the other dinosaurs for eggs before the angry mother could stop it. It also had long arms and strong hands, which could have been used for digging up roots or grabbing the small hairy mammals that scuttled past.

Horns and clubs
At the same time as *Struthiomimus* was racing around, there were a number of larger, heavier dinosaurs that had evolved various horns and clubs in order to protect themselves from even the fiercest of the flesh-eaters.

Ankylosaurus

Struthiomimus

Robinson.

Triceratops looked rather like an overgrown rhinoceros. It had a sharp horn on its nose, and, as if that were not enough, an even longer horn grew out of its skull above each eye. The back of the head and the neck were also protected by a great bony shield. If *Tyrannosaurus* tried to attack *Triceratops*, it would have met with a tough fight. *Triceratops* could easily give a fatal injury with its horns if a meat-eater came in too close. Many meat-eaters attack their prey by snapping at the back of the neck. That is often a weak fleshy area. However, this area was fully protected in *Triceratops*.

The ankylosaurs had found another solution to defense. At first, these large dinosaurs look like huge turtles. They have rows of bony plates set into the skin over the back and sides, and over the top of the skull. Sometimes there are rows of spikes around the side as well. *Ankylosaurus* was over 30 feet long, and about the size and shape of a military tank. If *Tyrannosaurus* had tried to sink its fangs into *Ankylosaurus* it would simply have broken them off. *Ankylosaurus* could also have counterattacked by swinging its tail. There was a great mass of bone at the end, which could have given a serious injury to any attacker.

Many of the dinosaurs of the late Cretaceous could survive an attack from great meat-eaters such as Tyrannosaurus. *The ostrich dinosaurs, such as* Struthiomimus, *could run very fast, while the ceratopsian* Triceratops *and the ankylosaur* Ankylosaurus *had strong armor and weapons.*

67

The helmet heads

Some of the strangest of the Cretaceous dinosaurs were a group of ornithopods called the hadrosaurs. They are also known as "duckbills," because of their broad duck-like snouts, or "helmet-heads," as they often had strange crests or helmets on the top of their heads.

The duckbills browsed on the low vegetation and small trees found around lakes. Some skeletons of these dinosaurs have been found with plant remains in their stomach area, and these show that they ate leaves from conifer trees.

Some scientists have suggested that the duckbills spent all of their time on the dry land, while others think that they swam around in the water most of the time. They might have had webbed feet, and they were probably good swimmers. It was thought that this might have been their way of escaping from the great meat-eaters like *Tyrannosaurus*. However, there was nothing to stop *Tyrannosaurus* from swimming as well.

One of the most remarkable of the "helmets" belonged to the 30-foot long *Parasaurolophus* from the late Cretaceous of North America. Scientists once thought that its crest was a tube that allowed *Parasaurolophus* to

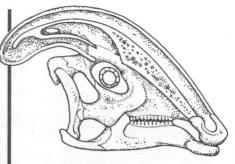

The skull of this female Parasaurolophus *shows the air tubes that ran right to the end of its crest.*

A small herd of Parasaurolophus *feed on the leaves of early pine trees on the shores of a late Cretaceous lake.*

Right: this amazing cast of a hatching duckbill shows that these baby dinosaurs were quite small and defenseless. Its parents would have fed and cared for it until it grew old enough to look after itself.

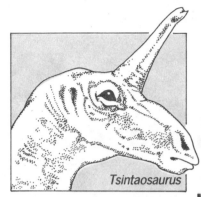

Tsintaosaurus

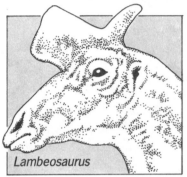

Lambeosaurus

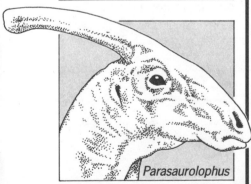

Parasaurolophus

The different duckbills can be told apart by the shape of their helmets — from spines that point forward to flat bony lumps like a dinner plate set on end. The male Parasaurolophus's *crest (shown above) was longer than the female's (see skull shown opposite).*

breathe underwater. However, we now know that there is no air hole at the end of the crest.

When the skull is cut open, it turns out that the long crest has air passages inside that run up from the nostril, and then back down into the throat. When *Parasaurolophus* breathed, the air passed all the way to the end of the crest, and all the way down again. Why should this happen?

Recently, some scientists made models of the skull of *Parasaurolophus*. When they blew into the back air tubes, the model made a noise like a trumpet. They suggested that when *Parasaurolophus* breathed out very hard, the air rushed through the tubes in the crest and it made a great bellowing noise. Each species of duckbilled dinosaur had a different kind of helmet head, and so each species would have made a different kind of noise when it breathed out. The late Cretaceous world was filled with high-pitched squeaks, low honks, and great bellows as the duckbills talked to each other.

A dinosaur nursery

Recent finds in Montana include the nests, eggs, and babies of the duckbilled dinosaur *Maiasaura*. It seems that these dinosaurs built large nests on the ground by scooping out a hollow in the earth, about 6½ feet across. The *Maiasaura* mother then laid from 20 to 25 eggs in the nest, and covered them with soil to keep them warm. Some weeks later, the young duckbills hatched. They were very tiny, and it seems that the mother dinosaur looked after the young until they were big enough to feed themselves.

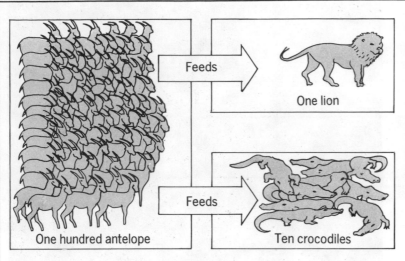

Feeds

One lion

Feeds

One hundred antelope

Ten crocodiles

A WARM-BLOODED APPETITE?

Warm-blooded lions must eat ten times as much as cold-blooded crocodiles in order to keep their bodies warm. Figures suggest that dinosaurs were more like lions than crocodiles, but are these numbers accurate enough?

Were dinosaurs warm-blooded?

All mammals and birds are warm-blooded. Even on a very cold day, our bodies stay warm. However, a reptile like a lizard or a tortoise cannot keep its body warm in cold temperatures.

Until about 1970, most scientists had assumed that the dinosaurs were **cold-blooded**, like the reptiles. However, various scientists suggested that the dinosaurs must have had constant body temperatures at all times. How can we tell, when the dinosaurs have all been dead for millions of years?

When scientists took slices of bones from modern mammals and from dinosaurs, they found that the dinosaur bone was much more like a cow's bone than a lizard's bone. This suggested that the dinosaurs were

Dinosaur bone looks more like cow bone than lizard bone under the microscope. Does this mean that dinosaurs were warm-blooded, or does it simply tell us that they were big?

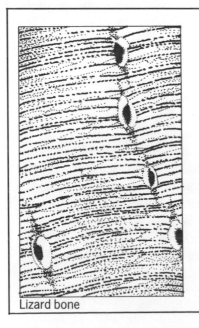

Lizard bone

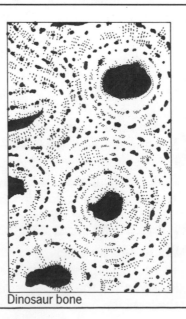

Dinosaur bone

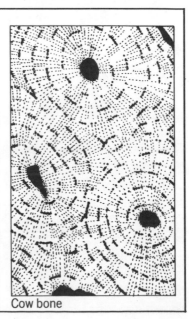

Cow bone

warm-blooded, just as cows are, rather than cold-blooded like lizards. Other scientists did not agree. They said that the type of bone seen in dinosaurs and cows was the result of their large size. Lizards only have different types of bones because they are small. It turns out that large living reptiles like crocodiles and sea turtles also have the cow-type bone. So dinosaur bone does not prove that they were warm-blooded.

Then the scientists looked at the numbers of meat-eaters and the numbers of plant-eaters. Today, a warm-blooded meat-eater like a lion has to eat ten times as much as a cold-blooded meat-eater like a crocodile. So, on a grassy plain in Africa, you will always find fewer lions than crocodiles living around a herd of antelope. When scientists counted the number of meat-eating dinosaurs and plant-eating dinosaurs, they found the number of meat-eaters was very low. This gave them the "warm-blooded" figures. Other scientists argued that the figures were not accurate enough.

It is unlikely that anyone will ever know whether the dinosaurs were warm-blooded or not. The larger dinosaurs probably kept constant body temperatures in any case just because they were so big. So they could be both cold-blooded and warm-blooded at the same time!

The bodies of dinosaurs look more like modern mammals than reptiles. Ankylosaurus *stood upright, just as a rhinoceros does today. This means that they probably also ran like mammals and so might have been warm-blooded as well in order to keep up their speed of movement.*

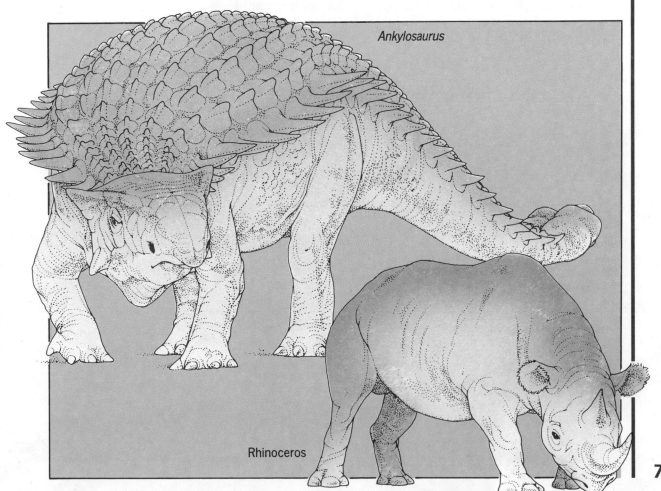

Ankylosaurus

Rhinoceros

The end of the dinosaurs

Why did the dinosaurs disappear? At the end of the Cretaceous, there were as many dinosaurs as there ever had been. Rocks from this period are rich with fossils of the great meat-eaters like *Tyrannosaurus*, and a huge range of plant-eaters such as the helmet-heads, the horned ceratopsians, and the massive ankylosaurs. Yet the next layer of rocks has no dinosaurs at all.

The death of the dinosaurs is one of the many mass extinctions that have taken place during the history of life. Any explanation for the death of the dinosaurs also has to explain why many other animals disappeared at the same time. In the sea, many tiny microscopic animals and some important swimming shellfish, the **ammonites** and **belemnites**, died out. The great sea reptiles — the ichthyosaurs, plesiosaurs, and **mosasaurs** — and the flying pterosaurs also disappeared. However, some groups were hardly affected at all. The plants, snails, frogs, lizards, birds, and mammals carried on as if nothing had happened.

One suggestion is that the climate was becoming cooler. The warm lush forests that the dinosaurs knew gradually disappeared. As these tropical forests became

Above: the last dinosaurs do not look like a weakened group of animals about to die out.

smaller, the dinosaurs followed them toward the equator until there were hardly any left. At the same time, cooler forests moved south from the Arctic Circle, and the fur-covered mammals came with them. After five or six million years of gradual change, the dinosaurs had all gone, and the mammals had taken over. The cooler weather also affected the seas, and the water became colder. The ammonites, plesiosaurs, and mosasaurs lost the warmth that they liked, and they gradually dwindled and disappeared.

The other theory is that the earth was hit by great meteorites or comets from outer space. This happened very suddenly and there were great explosions. Huge clouds of dust were blown into the sky and were carried all around the world by the wind. The great dust cloud blacked out the sun, and the freezing world was covered with darkness. The dinosaurs all died immediately and so did the other animals in the sea. After a year or so, the dust cloud cleared and life carried on, but the dinosaurs, ammonites, and plesiosaurs had all gone. Only the furry mammals, feathered birds, and hibernating crocodiles, turtles, lizards, and snails survived.

It is hard to be sure which theory is correct at the moment. For the present, the death of the dinosaurs remains one of the great mysteries of the history of life.

The last days of the dinosaurs. Most of the animals shown here — the giant crocodile, frogs, birds, mammals, plants, and insects — survived the mass extinction. The dinosaurs alone in this scene were doomed.

5. In Air and Sea

Back to the ocean

As the age of the dinosaurs began, some groups of reptiles went back to the seas while others took to flying in the air. Many of these died out at the same time as the dinosaurs. A number of unusual kinds of fish and shellfish also appeared and died out during this time.

Permian seas were filled with primitive bony fish and sharks, as well as the coiled swimming shellfish called nautiloids and **ammonoids**. These shellfish are related to the modern octopus and squid, and they swam by forcing out jets of water to make them shoot backward.

The first fish-eating reptiles also lived in the Permian. These included the small, 16-inch long *Mesosaurus*. This lizardlike animal had long narrow jaws lined with needle-sharp teeth that it used to spear fish. It had broad hands and paddlelike feet, and a long flat tail that it could have used for swimming.

The small fish-eating reptile Mesosaurus *tries to attack an ammonite. The ammonite squirts out a cloud of inky material to confuse its attacker, while it makes its escape. Skeletons of* Mesosaurus *have been found in Africa and in South America.*

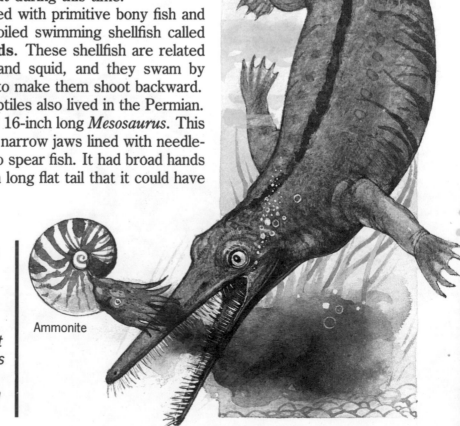

Mesosaurus

Ammonite

Nothosaur

Ichthyosaur

Placodont

Sea reptiles became much more varied as the Mesozoic age began. The **nothosaurs** were small, active animals, about 3 feet long. It is easy to see how the nothosaurs evolved from land animals: They still had four strong legs, and they could have easily crawled out of the sea to hunt or to lay eggs.

The dolphinlike ichthyosaurs, on the other hand, had become fully adapted to life in the sea. They had evolved from land animals of some sort, but no one knows quite which group. The ichthyosaurs appeared at the very beginning of the Triassic, and they were already fully fish-shaped. Their feet had changed into paddles by becoming shorter and flatter. All the arm and hand bones of a land animal were still there, but they had changed shape and become covered over by thick skin to form a paddle. Their smooth bodies cut easily through the water, helped by the big fins on their tails and backs. Ichthyosaurs fed on fish, which they could easily catch because they were such fast swimmers themselves.

Reptiles of the Triassic seas. A long-snouted nothosaur paddles along at the surface, above the dolphin-like ichthyosaur and shell-crushing placodont.

75

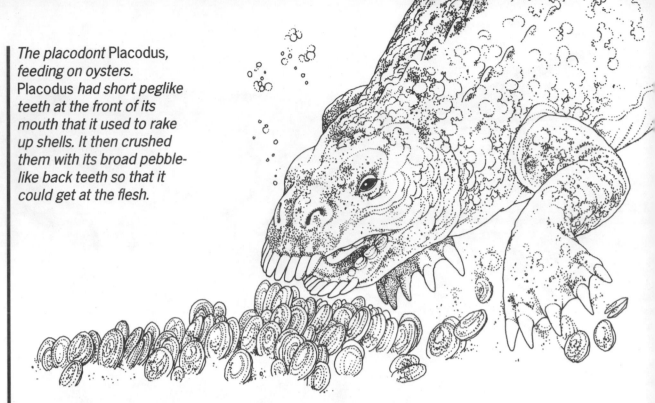

The placodont Placodus, *feeding on oysters.* Placodus *had short peglike teeth at the front of its mouth that it used to rake up shells. It then crushed them with its broad pebble-like back teeth so that it could get at the flesh.*

The shell-crushers

The third and strangest group of Triassic sea reptiles were the **placodonts**. These were 6½ to 10 feet long, with broad heads and huge, paddlelike feet. Their teeth were remarkable. There were hard, pebblelike teeth on the jaws and the roof of the mouth, while the front teeth were longer and more like the teeth on a rake. The placodont probably fed on shellfish like oysters, which were fixed to the rocks in shallow water. It scraped them off with its front teeth, and took a few shells into its mouth. It ground these up with its great rounded teeth and spat out the shell fragments. It could then swallow the flesh.

The ammonoids

Many new groups of shellfish appeared in the Triassic seas. These included many types that placodonts may have eaten, such as the first oysters and limpets. The ammonoids also became important. These all lived in coiled shells, and they swam about in the open water well above the seabed. The ammonoids had large eyes and tentacles, just like their living relatives, the squids and octopuses. There were dozens of different ammonoids during the Triassic, and their fossil shells are quite common.

Tanystropheus — long-necked fish-eater

One of the strangest of the Triassic reptiles was *Tanystropheus*, which probably lived along the seashore. *Tanystropheus* was up to 20 feet long, but more than half of this length was taken up by its neck. The remarkable

The fossil shell of Ceratites, *a typical ammonoid of the Triassic seas.*

76

Tanystropheus

thing about this very long neck was that it had only 11 bones. This meant that although its neck was as long as a large snake, it could not bend it around in a snakelike way.

Tanystropheus had a small head, and its jaws were lined with sharp little teeth. It seems that it ate fish and ammonoids, possibly by standing on rocks at the side of the sea and by darting its head into the water from above — in a similar way that seabirds look for fish from the air and then dive down quickly to catch them.

Although skeletons of adult *Tanystropheus* have been found in various parts of Europe in rocks that were formed in shallow seas, skeletons of its young seem to have been found in rocks that were laid down on land. It has been suggested that the young reptiles might have fed on insects until their necks had grown long enough to hunt for fish.

The nothosaurs, placodonts, and tanystropheids all disappeared at the end of the Triassic period, at the same time that the rhynchosaurs and various mammallike reptiles died out on land. The ichthyosaurs and the ammonoids were also heavily hit, and nearly vanished altogether. However, a few lines lived on into the Jurassic period when they again became important in the seas.

Jurassic giants

The Mesozoic seas of the giant reptiles were very different from those of today. Geologists believe that the waters were warm in most parts of the world, because there was no ice at the North or South Poles. Fish and animals of tropical reefs lived in a larger part of the ocean than they do now, and it seems likely that the great sea reptiles could swim freely all over the world.

The plesiosaurs were the giants of the warm Jurassic seas. They evolved from the nothosaurs of the Triassic, but they were bigger and better built for life in the water than their ancestors. They generally had long necks, and four strong paddles that were used in swimming. Plesiosaurs might have been able to move on land as well. They hunted by darting their long necks into shoals of fish and snatching them up with their sharp teeth.

The fossil bones of this ichthyosaur are so well preserved that the large eye socket, the long jaws, and the rounded bones of the paddle can all be clearly seen. This fossil also has a trace of the outline of the body, showing the shape of the tail fin, the fin on the back, and the dolphin-shaped body.

Ichthyosaur fossil

Ichthyosaurus

Metriorhynchus

PLESIOSAUR PADDLES

Plesiosaurs swam by using their paddles. Some scientists suggested that they used them like the oars of a boat, while others thought that they moved them in a great figure eight, as sea turtles do today. It now seems that plesiosaurs swam in the way that penguins do, by "flying" through the water.

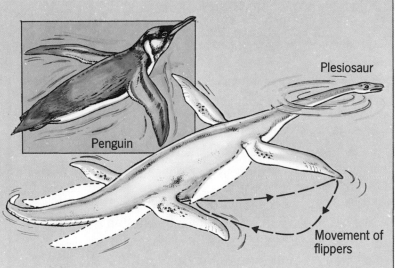

Penguin

Plesiosaur

Movement of flippers

The ichthyosaurs were also very important in the Jurassic. Some were only 3 feet long, but the largest were twelve times bigger. Fossilized ichthyosaur droppings have been found, which show what these fishlike reptiles ate. Some show fish spines and scales, and others contain parts of ammonoids and other shellfish.

The **pliosaurs** were a special type of plesiosaur. They were huge, bulky animals with short necks and long powerful jaws. Some pliosaurs were as long as 40 feet, and they probably fed on smaller sea reptiles.

The first crocodiles were land animals that had appeared during the Triassic. In the Jurassic, some of them took to the seas, where they became well suited to the ocean life. Many had long snouts lined with sharp teeth for catching fish. Some even had paddles instead of feet, and fins on their tails to help them swim faster.

A scene in a Jurassic sea. The ichthyosaur Ichthyosaurus *and the plesiosaur* Cryptocleidus *swim near the surface, while the giant pliosaur* Liopleurodon *clamps its jaws around the small sea crocodile* Metriorhynchus.

Cryptocleidus

Liopleurodon

Elasmosaurs and mosasaurs

The ichthyosaurs, plesiosaurs, and crocodiles that had filled the Jurassic seas gradually became less common in the Cretaceous. One of the new groups that took their place were the **elasmosaurs**. These huge reptiles were up to 43 feet long, with tiny heads and very long necks that were longer than the rest of the body. They darted their heads from side to side to seize fish. A typical elasmosaur, like *Elasmosaurus*, had 76 bones in its neck. This made the neck much more flexible and snakelike than the neck of the Triassic *Tanystropheus*.

The giant pliosaurs were still important in the Cretaceous. One of the biggest was *Kronosaurus* from Australia, which was 56 feet long — in other words, the size of a large whale. Its head was as big as a large car.

Some of the reptiles that lived in Cretaceous times. A mosasaur swims at the surface, above the large sea turtle Archelon. A long-necked elasmosaur darts its head at a small shoal of fish. Some ammonites in their coiled shells swim past at the bottom right.

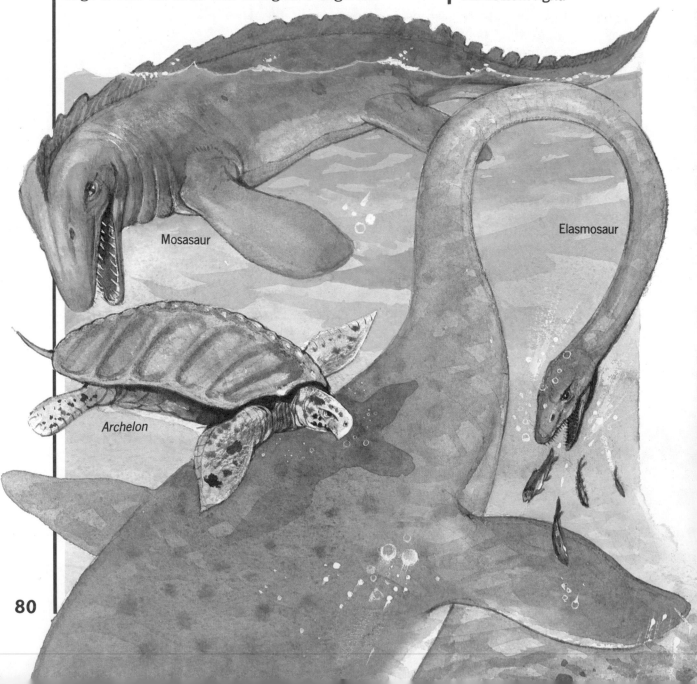

Mosasaur

Elasmosaur

Archelon

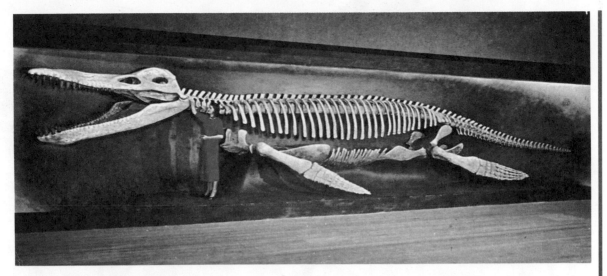

Mosasaurs and turtles

A completely new group of fish-eating reptiles in the Cretaceous were the mosasaurs. The giant skull of one of these sea monsters caused a sensation when it was discovered in Holland in the 18th century, and later led to an international incident. This took place a few years after the French Revolution, when French troops marched into Holland. They shelled the town of Maastricht, where the "Maas reptile's" skull was kept. The troops were under strict instructions to find the skull, and the twelve soldiers who eventually hauled it back to Paris were rewarded with 600 bottles of wine.

The mosasaurs were as huge as the pliosaurs. They had enormous heads, and the bigger ones probably fed on other marine reptiles. The smaller ones fed on shellfish, such as ammonites and belemnites. These were relatives of the Triassic *ammonoids*, and were very plentiful in Cretaceous seas. The ammonites lived inside coiled shells, while the belemnites had a bullet-shaped shell inside their body. They probably looked like modern squid, with large eyes and many tentacles. The shell inside provided a sort of backbone that supported the soft body.

Another new group of reptiles in Cretaceous seas were the turtles. A large late Cretaceous turtle called *Archelon* fed on fish in the surface waters over parts of North America.

All of the sea monsters that lived during the age of the dinosaurs died out at the end of the Cretaceous period, at the time of the great mass extinction. Only the turtles were to survive.

The skeleton of the giant pliosaur Kronosaurus *from Australia. This giant reptile was the size of a whale, and it could have eaten any fish or reptile in the Cretaceous oceans.*

Ammonite

The giant Cretaceous pterosaur Pteranodon *may have glided out over the sea to catch fish. The crest on the back of its head may have been used to balance the great beak at the front.*

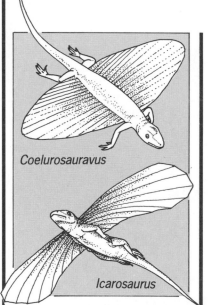

Coelurosauravus

Icarosaurus

Two early reptile gliders. Coelurosauravus *came from the late Permian of Africa, and* Icarosaurus *is known from the late Triassic of North America. Both had "wings" made from skin stretched over very long ribs. These two reptiles could not fly, but they glided from tree to tree.*

Into the air

The first flying animals were the insects that came on the scene in the Devonian and became very varied in the Carboniferous period. However, it was not until the Permian that the first reptiles took to the air.

The first "flying" reptiles could not really fly. They simply glided. These include *Coelurosauravus* from the late Permian of Africa and Germany. *Coelurosauravus* was a small lizardlike animal with very long ribs that stuck out at the side of its body. The ribs were covered with a thin skin. This allowed *Coelurosauravus* to glide from tree to tree. It could not flap these "wings," but they allowed it to cover much greater distances than an animal without any wings at all.

These early gliders died out at the end of the Permian, and there were no more flying reptiles until the late Triassic. It was then that a whole range of reptiles started flying again. There were forms like *Icarosaurus* from North America. Its wings were of a different shape to those of *Coelurosauravus*, and they could be folded back out of the way when *Icarosaurus* was not gliding. It is likely that these early gliders leaped through the trees, snatching at insects in midair.

Wings of skin

The pterosaurs were the first reptiles that could actually fly by flapping their wings. Some recent discoveries in northern Italy have now shown that they were first

around in the late Triassic, and it seems likely that they evolved from the ancestors of dinosaurs.

The pterosaurs became very common in the Jurassic. Many of them were the size of pigeons or crows, and they probably flew about in just the same way, feeding on insects and other small animals. Some fossils of pterosaurs show that they had hair, which suggests that they were fully warm-blooded, just as birds and mammals are today.

The pterosaurs had long thin arm bones, and one of the fingers was especially long. These bones formed the front edge of the wing, which was made from skin like the wings of modern bats. The bones of pterosaurs were hollow, which made them light in the air.

Giant wings

The largest pterosaurs lived in Cretaceous North America. *Pteranodon* had a wing span of up to 23 feet, making it much bigger than any living bird. In 1976, an even larger pterosaur was found in Texas. It was called *Quetzalcoatlus*, meaning "feathered serpent." The skeleton of *Quetzalcoatlus* is not complete, but scientists guess that it had a wing span of 40 to 50 feet. Like many of the later pterosaurs, it had a long neck and no tail. It was the size of a small airplane, and it may even have been too big to fly. However, its body was quite small, and it was probably able to glide and soar on currents of air, as a glider does today.

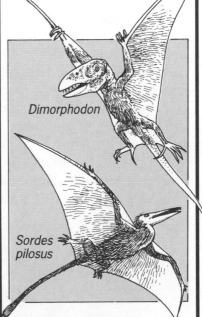

Dimorphodon

Sordes pilosus

The Jurassic pterosaur Dimorphodon, *with its sharp biting teeth and long tail, looks like something out of a Dracula film.* Sordes pilosus *was just as ugly, as its Latin name — meaning "hairy filth" — suggests.*

83

THE BIRDS AND PTEROSAURS

Birds arose from small lizard-hipped dinosaurs like *Coelophysis*. The origin of the flying pterosaurs is not clear, but they were a completely separate group. One recent suggestion is that the pterosaurs arose from the same ancestors as the dinosaurs.

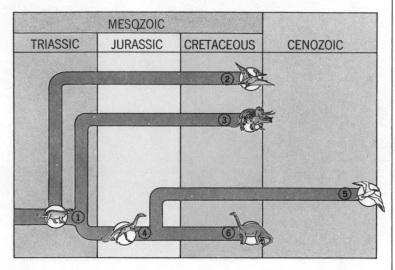

The birds

The first birds appeared after all the other gliders and pterosaurs had come on the scene. The oldest known bird is one of the most famous fossils in the world, and it is very important in evolution.

Ancient wings

In 1861, some workers in a limestone quarry of late Jurassic age in southern Germany discovered a fossilized feather. Every detail could be seen, and it looked just like a feather from a modern bird. A few months after this, a complete skeleton was found of an animal about the size of a pigeon. All of the thin delicate bones could be seen, and all around the body were dozens of beautifully preserved feathers. The fossil was named *Archaeopteryx*, which means "ancient wing."

The fossil quickly became very famous because it was obviously the oldest known bird in the world. It was

Key to bird and pterosaur evolution:
1. Thecodonts
2. Pterosaurs
3. Bird-hipped dinosaurs
4. *Coelophysis*
5. Birds
6. Lizard-hipped dinosaurs

Are the birds the living survivors of the dinosaurs? Without its feathers, Archaeopteryx *would have looked very like a tiny meat-eating dinosaur such as* Compsognathus.

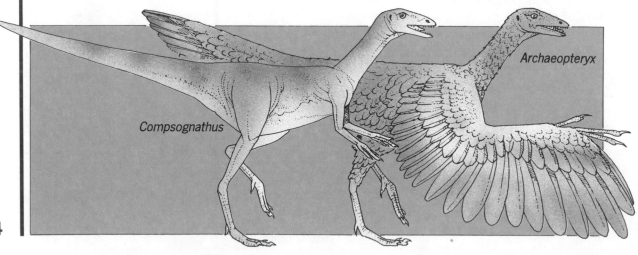

Compsognathus

Archaeopteryx

bought by the British Museum in London for a very large sum of money. A second very good skeleton was found in 1877, and it was bought by a museum in Berlin. Since then, another three skeletons of *Archaeopteryx* have been found, each with impressions of feathers scattered around the bones.

The scientists who first looked at *Archaeopteryx* saw that it was a very primitive bird. It certainly had feathers and a wishbone (a special bone in the shoulder that only birds have). However, it also had a scaly head with a beak full of sharp little teeth, claws on its wings, and a long bony tail — all reptilelike features that modern birds have since lost. It seems then that *Archaeopteryx* is a **missing link** between reptiles and birds, just as some of the later mammallike reptiles are missing links between reptiles and mammals.

What group of reptiles did *Archaeopteryx* come from? There has been much discussion of this question by scientists recently. It seems now that *Archaeopteryx* is most like one of the small meat-eating dinosaurs such as *Coelophysis* from the Triassic or the tiny *Compsognathus* from the Late Jurassic of Germany. Indeed, it has been said that if *Archaeopteryx* had been found without any feathers at all, it might just as easily have been classified as a dinosaur!

The second Archaeopteryx *fossil was found in 1877, and is now in the Natural History Museum in Berlin. The feathers of the wings and on either side of the long bony tail can be seen quite clearly.*

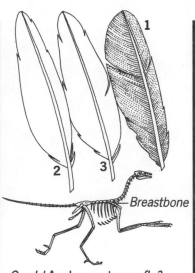

Could Archaeopteryx *fly? Fossils show that its feathers (1) were like those of modern birds that fly (2) rather than those that cannot fly (3). However, some scientists argue that its breastbone was too small and weak for flight.*

Could Archaeopteryx fly?

Some scientists have suggested recently that *Archaeopteryx* could not fly. If this is the case, it is odd that it should have feathers and wings! It is true that *Archaeopteryx* does not have a deep breastbone, as modern birds do. The breastbone is where the powerful wing muscles are attached — as you can see in any cooked chicken. However, bats do not have a deep breastbone either, and they can fly well enough.

Scientists have also looked at the feathers of *Archaeopteryx* in great detail. These turn out to be just like the feathers of modern flying birds. Modern birds that do not fly, like ostriches, have quite different feathers.

Airborne dinosaurs

There are two theories about how the first bird-dinosaurs actually started to fly. Did they do it by dashing along the ground at great speed, and leaping up in the air to snatch at insects? Even quite small wings in an early form would have allowed it to leap higher. The other idea is that birds learned to fly "from the trees down" rather than "from the ground up." An early dinosaur may have moved into the trees and developed long sharp claws (like those

Hesperornis

Ichthyornis

found on *Archaeopteryx*) to hang on to the bark and branches. Wings of any kind would have been useful in gliding at first, and later in proper flapping flight.

Giant fish-eaters

Archaeopteryx is the only bird known in the Jurassic. However, several different birds had appeared by Cretaceous times. Some of the best known come from North America, from the same rocks as the giant pterosaurs like *Pteranodon*.

Hesperornis was a giant diving bird about 6½ feet long. It seems to have lost its powers of flight, and it hunted fish by diving. It might have been able to swim for long distances underwater, as living penguins do. Another late Cretaceous bird is the smaller *Ichthyornis*, which looked rather like a seagull. It was probably also a fish-eater that hunted by flying low over the waves and diving in to seize any fish it saw near the surface.

Hesperornis and *Ichthyornis* were primitive in one way: They still had teeth. However, various modern types of birds arose in the late Cretaceous that had no teeth, and the toothed birds died out during the great mass extinction.

During the late Cretaceous in Kansas, the large diving bird Hesperornis *swam on the surface of the sea, while the smaller* Ichthyornis *flew above. These birds lived at the same time as the giant pterosaurs like* Pteranodon, *shown in the background.*

Pteranodon

6. The Age of Mammals

After the dinosaurs

After the dinosaurs died out, the world must have seemed a very empty place. There were hardly any large animals on land at all. There were birds, lizards, crocodiles, and turtles, and a few rat-sized and cat-sized hairy animals. These creatures were the mammals, which had lived in the undergrowth during the whole of the age of the dinosaurs. They had first come on the scene back in Triassic times, but had been overshadowed for millions of years by the dinosaurs. Now that the dinosaurs had all died out, their chance had come.

By Paleocene times, the Atlantic Ocean had still not fully opened up. However, from Paleocene times onward, the mammals began to evolve into special groups that varied from continent to continent.

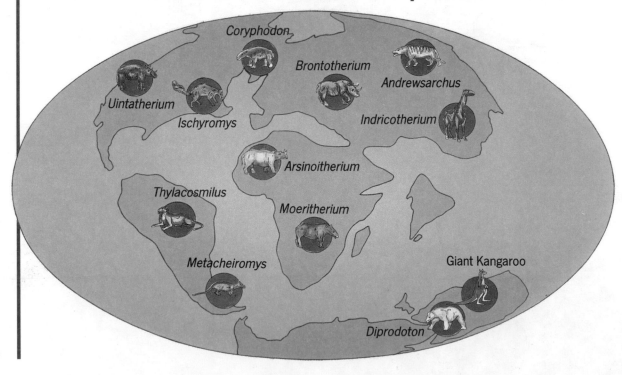

Paleocene mammals

The age of the mammals began at the start of the Cenozoic era. The word "Cenozoic" means "new life," and the time it covers dates from the death of the dinosaurs to the present day. The first of the Cenozoic epochs was the Paleocene. At this time, the continents were still attached to each other in places. Europe and North America were joined over Greenland, and Antarctica and Australia were still joined in the south. This allowed the early mammals to travel over much of the world quite easily.

The mammals of the Paleocene included early hedgehogs and shrews and primitive monkeylike animals such as *Plesiadapis*. There were even gliding animals like *Planetotherium*. Some larger mammals appeared during late Paleocene times, such as the plant-eaters *Barylambda* and *Taeniolabis*.

A scene in the Paleocene woods. Planetotherium *(top left) glides between the trees on skin webs between its tail and legs. Behind it is the pony-sized plant-eater* Barylambda, *and sitting on the branch is the long-tailed* Plesiadapis. Taeniolabis *(bottom right) was the size of a beaver, and ate nuts and fruit. In the bottom left of the picture is an early shrew.*

WHAT IS A MAMMAL?

Unlike reptiles, mammals have hair all over their bodies that helps to keep their temperature constant. They have much larger brains, and complicated passages in their noses that warm the air they breathe. Reptiles lay eggs, but mammals give birth to live young.

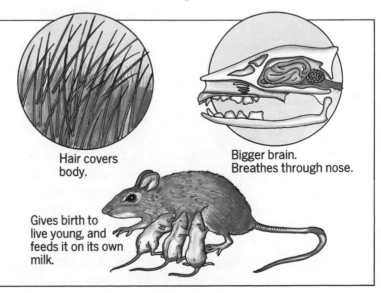

Hair covers body.

Bigger brain. Breathes through nose.

Gives birth to live young, and feeds it on its own milk.

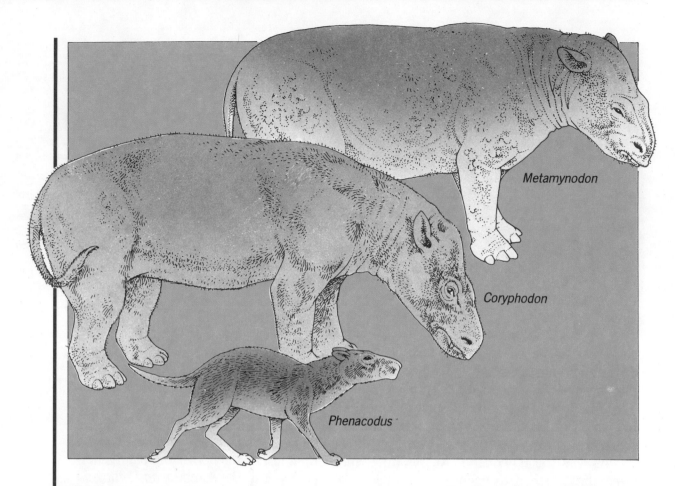

Metamynodon

Coryphodon

Phenacodus

Bulky plant-eaters

The next Cenozoic epoch, the Eocene, had warm climates in many parts of the world. In the lush forests of these times, the mammals became very varied and important. *Phenacodus* was about the size of a large dog, with a long body and short legs. Its head was long and it had a square snout. It had five toes on its hands and feet, but instead of nails these had small hooves that allowed it to run fast.

A larger Eocene plant-eater was the slow, heavily built *Coryphodon*. It was over 10 feet long, with broad spreading feet and long tusks, rather like those of a wild pig. It has been suggested that *Coryphodon* might have spent a great deal of its time in shallow water, feeding on plants around the edges of ponds.

Metamynodon was an early type of rhinoceros. It was a large, fat animal with short legs, and it probably fed on pond plants just as *Coryphodon* did.

The first horses also appeared in the Eocene. Little *Hyracotherium* was only about the size of a terrier, but later horses soon became larger and more like their modern relatives. *Hyracotherium* lived in Europe and North America, feeding on the leaves of the warm forests.

One of the most remarkable groups of Eocene plant-eaters were the **uintatheres**, such as *Uintatherium*.

Three early plant-eating mammals of the Eocene. Metamynodon and Coryphodon were quite large, and they may have lived partly in the water as hippopotamuses do today. Phenacodus was much smaller, and is related to modern horses, cattle, pigs, and deer.

This large animal was 6½ feet high at the shoulder and up to 13 feet long. It had bony knobs all over its body, and very long tusks. The knobs may have been used like horns in fighting, and the tusks were probably used for raking up plant food. The uintatheres were the biggest animals on land in the Eocene, but the group died out before the era was over and left no living relatives.

Flightless giants

The Eocene meat-eaters were a strange mixture. There were some meat-eating mammals related to modern cats and some related to dogs. Some hunted on the ground and others hunted in the trees.

However, the most unusual of the meat-eaters were the giant flightless birds. *Diatryma* was more than 6½ feet high. It could run very fast on its hind legs, and seize plant-eating mammals such as *Phenacodus* and early horses in its great beak. Like modern birds, *Diatryma* had no teeth, but the beak was sharp and horny enough for slicing up its prey.

Bats

The first bat, *Icaronycteris*, is known from the Eocene. It had wings and it could clearly fly very well. It had small pointed teeth and fed on insects — probably at night when birds cannot see well enough to hunt.

This first bat is so like its modern relatives that it does not give us many clues about how bats appeared in the first place. They must have evolved in the Paleocene from some small tree-climbing, shrewlike animal, but no one knows yet quite how this happened.

Diatryma

Hyracotherium

The giant meat-eating bird Diatryma *could probably have run as fast as a modern ostrich. It might well have preyed on the small early horses of the Eocene such as* Hyracotherium.

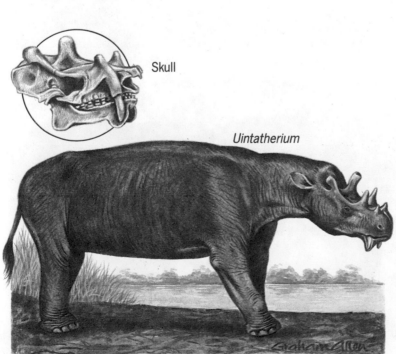

Skull

Uintatherium

The giant plant-eater Uintatherium *is known from the Eocene of the United States. This was the biggest mammal to have evolved by Eocene times, but the whole group disappeared at the end of the Eocene epoch. No one knows the reason for this.*

The story of the horse

One of the best-known stories in evolution is the history of the horse. The first horses appeared in the Eocene, 55 million years ago, and many hundreds of fossil horses have been collected in rocks from that date to the present day. The story of the horse was first worked out by paleontologists such as Edward Cope, during the 19th century.

The oldest horse was found as long ago as 1840 in England, and it was named *Hyracotherium*. *Hyracotherium* was also found later in North America where it was named *Eohippus*, or "dawn horse." However, the name *Hyracotherium* was given first, and it is used for both the English and the North American horses since they are nearly identical.

Horses of the forests and plains

Hyracotherium was only 12 inches high at the shoulder, although some of the later Eocene horses grew much larger. They lived deep within rich woodlands, feeding on leaves from trees and creeping about quietly among the bushes so as not to be caught by the meat-eaters. The horses in Europe died out at the end of the Eocene, and most of the rest of the story of the horse took place in North America.

The modern horse Equus *dwarfs its tiny ancestor* Hyracotherium. *In between are* Mesohippus *from the Oligocene,* Merychippus *and* Hypohippus *from the Miocene, and* Pliohippus *from the Pleistocene.*

Equus

Hypohippus

Pliohippus

Mesohippus

Merychippus

Hyracotherium

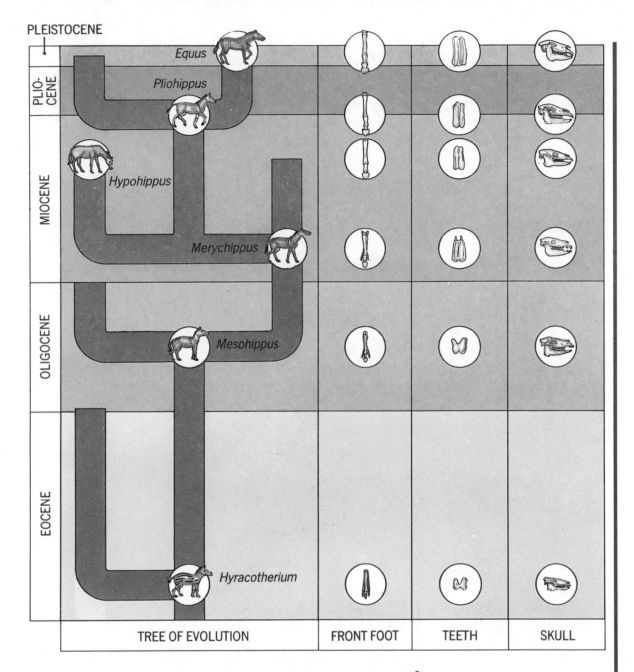

TREE OF EVOLUTION	FRONT FOOT	TEETH	SKULL

In the Oligocene epoch, which followed the Eocene, horses continued to grow bigger. *Mesohippus*, for example, was about the size of a greyhound. Later on in the Oligocene, the first grasses appeared and started to spread all over the world. Great open grasslands developed where there had once been forests to hide in. The early horses had either to adapt to their changing world or else die out.

The horses changed in three ways in the Oligocene and Miocene. Firstly, they became larger. *Merychippus* from the Miocene was 3 feet tall at the shoulder, while *Pliohippus* from the Pliocene reached 4 feet. (Modern horses measure 5 feet). Secondly, the horses grew longer legs and fewer toes. This allowed them to run faster to escape from meat-eaters on the open grassy plains.

The story of the horse is shown above in an evolutionary tree.
The main changes are to the front foot (less toes, from four to one), the teeth (becoming deeper), and the skull (longer, deeper jaws).
The horses evolved deeper jaws and longer teeth in order to grind up the new grasses, which were much tougher than the leaves of trees that Hyracotherium *and* Mesohippus *ate.*

93

Andrewsarchus

Patriofelis

Early meat-eaters of the Eocene. The giant "bear-dogs," called Andrewsarchus, *are tearing apart an early rhinoceros, while the catlike* Patriofelis *crouches hungrily nearby.*

Bear-dogs and brontotheres

Among the meat-eaters that prowled the late Eocene grasslands were the ancestors of the dog and the cat. The "bear-dog" *Andrewsarchus* had a huge skull with bone-crushing teeth. It may have eaten a mixed diet of flesh and plants, like a modern bear, but it could clearly have attacked the largest of the plant-eaters of its day. The smaller catlike *Patriofelis* could have hunted by creeping up on its prey and then pouncing suddenly. It had powerful shoulders and could have wrestled its prey to the ground. However, *Patriofelis* probably did not run very fast, and it relied more on its skill as a hunter to trap its food.

Both *Andrewsarchus* and *Patriofelis* died out in the Oligocene. True cats and dogs of a more modern type took their places. There were early dogs with long bodies and short legs, which hunted in packs, as many wild dogs do today. Cats of two types appeared: biting cats (like modern cats) and stabbing cats. The stabbing type, which have all died out now, include the saber-toothed cats. These had a pair of very long upper teeth that they could sink deep into the flesh of their prey. Stabbing cats of the Oligocene, and later times, could pierce the flesh of even the thickest-skinned plant-eaters.

Pigs and rhinos

The Oligocene was the age of the rhinoceros. The giant hornless *Baluchitherium* was the biggest land mammal of all time, reaching a height of 16 feet at the shoulder and a length of 26 feet. It probably weighed eight times as much as the largest living rhinoceros. *Baluchitherium* lived in Asia, and it could feed on the leaves of very tall trees that no other animal could reach.

The early pig *Archeotherium* had a large lumpy head, powerful shoulders, and long legs. It was clearly a fast runner, and it could probably defend itself from an attack by a meat-eater by using its massive tusks and bony head as a weapon.

The brontotheres

Unlike the early rhinoceroses and pigs, the **brontotheres** died out 30 million years ago. These were massive beasts with a peculiar catapult-shaped horn on their snouts. They lumbered over open plains, browsing on soft-leaved plants just as *Uintatherium* had done.

A pair of Brontotherium *lock horns in battle on a grassy Oligocene plain. These giant animals were more than twice the size of the warthoglike* Archeotherium.

Brontotherium

Archeotherium

Mammals of the sea

For a long time, biologists thought that whales and dolphins were giant fish. However, they are definitely mammals — they are warm blooded, they feed their young on milk, and they have hair (although not very much).

Like the reptiles of Mesozoic seas, the whales must have evolved from some land mammal that took to living in the water. Until recently, the oldest known whale was *Basilosaurus* from the Eocene of Africa. *Basilosaurus* was over 65 feet long. It was fully fitted out for an ocean life, with its smooth, serpentlike body and paddles instead of legs. The only clue to its origin lies in its teeth, which are broad and pointed like the early doglike meat-eaters. In 1980, an even older whale was found from the Eocene. *Pakicetus* was much smaller than *Basilosaurus*, being only about 3–5 feet long. Only a few skull bones of *Pakicetus* have been found so far, but it is likely that it had arms and legs that were halfway to becoming paddles. In the features of its skull, *Pakicetus* seems to be a good **missing link** between the doglike ancestors of whales and the true whales.

Early whales had broad dog-like teeth which suggest that they ate fish and other animals in the sea. The early whales probably moved into the sea to feed on the huge supply of food left after the extinction of the plesiosaurs, ichthyosaurs, and mosasaurs.

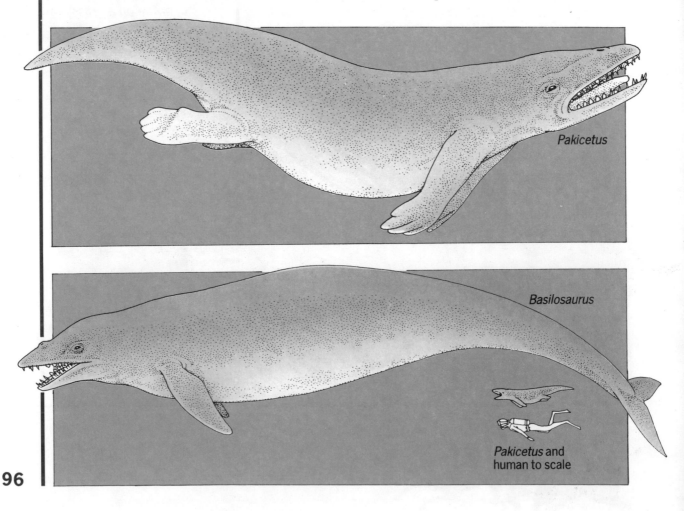

Pakicetus

Basilosaurus

Pakicetus and human to scale

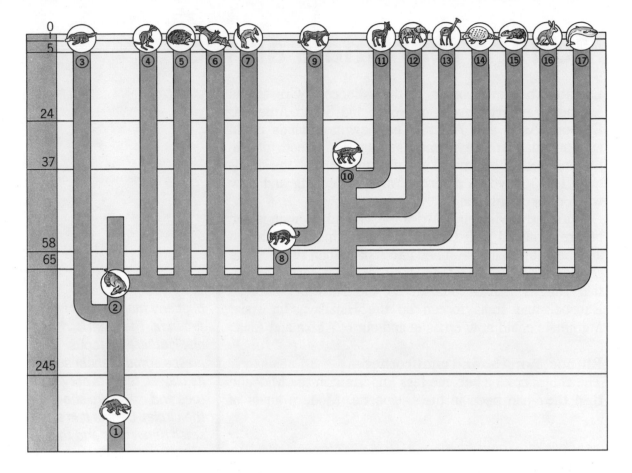

Mammal evolution

By Oligocene times, most of the modern groups of mammals had appeared. In fact, after the dinosaurs disappeared, it took the mammals only 10 million years or so to fill the world again with a huge range of new forms. From a scattering of small hairy animals came giant plant-eaters, meat-eaters, the whales in the seas, and the bats in the air.

The mammals are divided into three main groups. The most primitive, and rarest, are the **monotremes**. These include animals like the strange duckbilled platypus. The monotremes are still very reptilelike in a few features — they lay eggs, and they do not have good control of their body temperature.

The second group of mammals are the **marsupials**, such as the kangaroo, the koala, and the opossum. The marsupials produce live young instead of laying eggs, but the baby is so tiny when it is born that it has to grow up inside its mother's pouch before it can live outside.

The third group of mammals are the **placentals**, which include all the others. The placentals produce live young, which are often ready to walk as soon as they are born. The placentals today include all the familiar mammals such as mice, cats, horses, bats, and human beings.

Key to mammal evolution:
1. Mammallike reptiles
2. Mesozoic mammals
3. Monotremes
4. Marsupials
5. Insectivores
6. Bats
7. Primates
8. Creodonts (early meat-eaters)
9. Carnivores
10. Condylarths (early hoofed mammals)
11. Horses, rhinoceroses
12. Elephants
13. Pigs, cows, deer
14. Anteaters, sloths
15. Rodents
16. Rabbits, hares
17. Whales, dolphins

97

Modern mammals arrive

Climates became cooler in the Miocene. Grasslands spread over large areas of North and South America, Europe, Asia, and Africa. The new grasslands could support many more mammals than the forests of the Eocene and Oligocene. They also meant that the mammals had to evolve different ways of feeding and new ways of escaping danger.

During the Miocene, Africa (which had been an island before) collided with Europe and Asia. India (which had also been an island) bumped into Asia. When these island continents joined together, they forced up great mountain ranges. Africa pushed up the Alps in southern Europe, and India forced up the Himalayas in Asia. Mammals could now cross in and out of Africa and Asia.

Rhinos, horses, and chalicotheres

The rhinoceroses became less important in the Miocene than they had been in the Oligocene. Modern kinds of

Miocene mammals in North America. The great chalicothere Moropus *grasps some branches with its clawed feet (its curved toes and claws are shown in the circle). Behind it is a small rhinoceros and the giant horned rodent* Epigaulus.

Rhinoceros

Moropus

Epigaulus

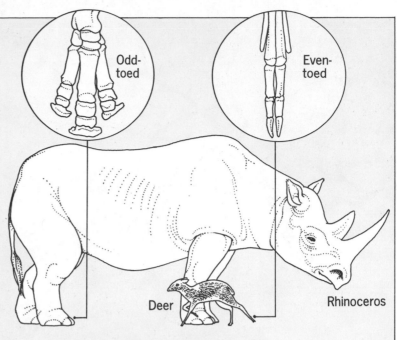

ODD AND EVEN TOES

All mammals originally had five toes on their hands and feet, just as we do. However, larger plant-eaters like horses and deer gradually evolved fewer toes so that they could run faster.

Today, plant-eaters are divided into two groups, depending on whether they have an odd number of toes (rhinos, horses) or an even number (cows, deer, hippos).

Odd-toed

Even-toed

Deer

Rhinoceros

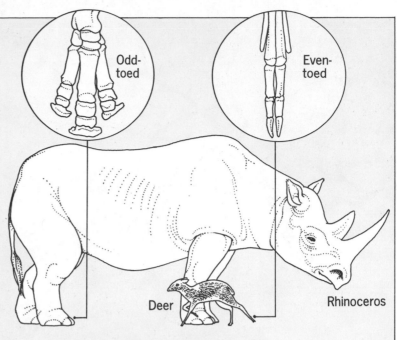

rhinos appeared in Africa and Asia – some with no horns, and others with either one or two horns on their snouts.

Horses such as *Merychippus* were very common on the great grasslands. Great herds roamed for large distances, and they could escape danger at high speed.

A very strange group of plant-eaters called the **chalicotheres** appeared in the Miocene of North America. These were distant relatives of the horses and rhinos, and they survived until about two million years ago. *Moropus* was the size of a large modern horse, but it did not have hooves. Its feet were fitted with large claws that were probably used for digging up roots. *Moropus* was clearly not a fast runner.

Giant horned rodents

It is often said that the most succesful mammals today are the rats and mice, because they seem to be able to live anywhere and eat anything. Rats and mice are examples of **rodents**, a group of mammals with strong front teeth that are used for gnawing at tough plants. Other rodents include beavers, hamsters, porcupines, and squirrels.

The first rodents appeared in the Eocene. These were generally small, tree-climbing animals rather like squirrels. Mice, rats, porcupines, and beavers had all appeared by Oligocene times.

One of the strangest early rodents was *Epigaulus* from the Miocene of North America. *Epigaulus* was about the size of a beaver, being 12 inches long. It had a powerful head with a small pair of bony horns on its snout. *Epigaulus* had strong front legs with great claws that it might have used to dig burrows.

Nimravides

Alticamelus

Synthetoceras

On a Miocene plain

The great grasslands of North America and Europe were home to a great variety of even-toed plant-eaters in the late Miocene. There were pigs of all shapes and sizes, including one with a horn on its nose. Other giant pigs lived in lakes and rivers. In the Pliocene, these giant pigs gave rise to the hippopotamuses in Africa.

Today, there are only two kinds of camels, in Africa and parts of Asia. In the Miocene there were dozens of species of camels even in North America and Europe. The large camel *Alticamelus* probably had no hump, but it did have a very long giraffelike neck that it used to feed on leaves high in the trees.

Cattle and deer

Cattle, antelope, and deer are the main plant-eaters in most parts of the world today. The ancestors of this successful group of animals first appeared in the Miocene.

The key to the success of these odd-toed plant-eaters is the way in which they digest their food. Horses and rhinos have to eat a great amount of plant material in order to keep alive, but cattle and deer have evolved special ways to get much more out of their food. When a cow swallows a mouthful of grass, the pieces are broken up by chemicals and bacteria in the first of its four

A scene from the grasslands of the late Miocene in North America. A pair of saber-toothed cats, Nimravides, *feed on a large pronghorn,* Synthetoceras. *In the background are a pair of long-necked camels,* Alticamelus, *and a small herd of early deer. Two bear-sized hunting dogs,* Amphicyon, *stand on the right.*

Amphicyon

stomachs. Any small stones or very tough pieces pass into the second stomach. The softer grass is then passed up to the mouth again where it is chewed up further. This is what is happening when a cow is "chewing the cud." It swallows this twice-chewed grass again and it passes into the third and then into the fourth stomach. Here it is completely broken down and the nutrients are taken out.

In the late Miocene and Pliocene, there were a number of strange horned even-toed plant-eaters. The antelope-like **pronghorns** were very common, and many of them had unusual horns either on their snouts or on top of their heads. *Synthetoceras* had a long forked horn on its nose, while other pronghorns had pairs of horns like spines, hooks, or broad leaves.

Cats and dogs

Cats, dogs, and bears were the main meat-eaters on the late Miocene plains. *Amphicyon*, a huge dog the size of a bear, could have attacked most of the plant-eaters of the time.

There were also early saber-toothed cats such as *Nimravides*. These had long stabbing teeth with which they could have cut through the thick skin of a plant-eater, and then allowed it to bleed to death. In this way, a saber-toothed cat could have killed a plant-eater that was much bigger than itself. The saber-tooths were an important group of large cats during the Pliocene and the Pleistocene, but they died out about 11,000 years ago.

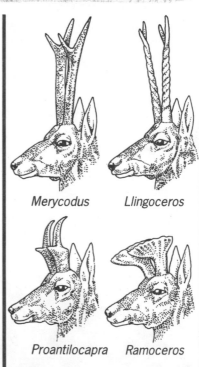

Merycodus   Llingoceros

Proantilocapra   Ramoceros

Four extinct pronghorns of the Miocene and Pliocene of North America. Today, only one species of pronghorn survives.

101

Trunks and tusks

Of all the species of elephants that bulldozed their way across the prehistoric landscape, only the African and the Indian survive today. Even these are rare, and we could be in danger of losing one of the most fascinating of all our modern mammals.

The first elephant appeared in the Eocene in Africa. This was *Moeritherium* — a small animal no larger than a pig. It had short tusks and it probably had no trunk. *Moeritherium* might have lived in swampy areas.

In the Oligocene the elephants split into two groups. On one line there was *Phiomia*, which was a little larger than *Moeritherium*. It had four short tusks — two in the upper jaw, and two in the lower. *Phiomia* might have had a short trunk, which it could have used for scooping up leaves and stuffing them into its mouth.

The elephants spread out

In the Miocene, Africa became joined to Europe and Asia and the elephants moved all over the world. Many different types evolved, and they all became much bigger. *Gomphotherium* lived in the Miocene of Asia, and *Platybelodon* lived in the Pliocene of North America. In both of these elephants, the lower pair of tusks formed a long shovellike snout that might have been used for digging up plants.

The second elephant line was much more important. *Deinotherium* lived in the Miocene of Africa, Asia, and Europe. It reached a height of 13 feet in some cases and had only two lower tusks that curved backward under its

Four early elephants: Phiomia from the Oligocene of Africa, Gomphotherium from the Miocene of Asia, Platybelodon from the Pliocene of North America, and Deinotherium from the Miocene of Africa, Europe, and Asia. The "shovel" tusks and "chin" tusks of the two Miocene forms show how varied the elephant group was in the past.

Gomphotherium

Phiomia

chin. These strange tusks might have been used for digging, and it is thought that *Deinotherium* might have had a long trunk, just like modern elephants.

Relatives of *Deinotherium* include the mastodons, mammoths, and modern elephants. The mastodons and mammoths lived during the Great Ice Age, and had a covering of thick hair in order to keep out the cold. They died out about 10,000 years ago, leaving only the elephants we see today in India and Africa.

Like their Indian relatives, the African elephants are only found in small herds today. They have been heavily hunted in the past for the ivory of their tusks.

Deinotherium

Platybelodon

South America — a different world

For millions of years, South America was an island. It only became joined to North America three or four million years ago. Until this time, the mammals in South America evolved quite separately from the mammals in other parts of the world, and many strange forms appeared.

Many of the South American marsupials were very different from the ones we know today. *Thylacosmilus* looked more like the saber-toothed cats that lived in other parts of the world, while *Borhyaena* looked like a dog. It was the size of a wolf, and it might have hunted its prey in packs across the great grassy plains.

Some special groups of plant-eaters also lived in South America at this time. *Astrapotherium* had a trunk and long chisellike tusks, although it was not a relation of the elephants. *Theosodon* was about the size of a small horse, and it might have had a trunk too. Its later relative *Macrauchenia* was larger, about the size of a camel, and great herds wandered across what is now Argentina, feeding on grasses and low bushes.

Thoatherium was very like a horse. It had long slender limbs, and it was about the same size as the Miocene horse from North America, *Mesohippus*. Another strange group were **toxodonts** like *Nesodon*, which was about the size of a heavily built sheep.

One particular South American group has survived to the present day. These are the **edentates** or "toothless

The mammals shown on this South American Miocene plain may look like dogs, horses, and elephants, but they are from different groups altogether. In the background, the doglike Borhyaena *hunts the camel-like* Theosodon, *while* Astrapotherium *searches for plants in a shallow pond. At the front, the horselike* Thoatherium *walks behind the heavy plant-eating* Nesodon.

Theosodon   Borhyaena   Toxodon   Astrapotherium   Thoatherium   Nesodon

Macrauchenia

Megatherium

Glyptodon

mammals." *Glyptodon* was a giant Pliocene armadillo. It was covered with a tough "shell" made from plates of bone and horn, and its spiky tail could be swung from side to side as a weapon. Another edentate was the large ground sloth *Megatherium*, which stood balanced on its hind legs and powerful tail in order to reach high into the trees. *Megatherium* used its long sharp claws to pull leaves down to eat.

A land bridge to the north

During the Pliocene, South America and North America became connected. North American mammals such as the mice, squirrels, bears, elephants, horses, and wolves moved south, and the South American mammals such as the opossums, armadillos, sloths, and toxodonts moved north. Some of the strange South American mammals died out very soon after this exchange, while others lived on until quite recently. The giant ground sloths died out only a few thousand years ago, and fossils of their reddish fur can still be found.

These mammals lived in the Pleistocene era in South America. Macrauchenia *was a strange long-necked animal with a trunk. The two others are edentates. The giant ground sloth* Megatherium *is related to the smaller tree sloths that live today, while the giant* Glyptodon *was a 13-foot long armadillo.*

105

The ice moves in

Ice and snow began to gather over the North Pole at the beginning of the Pleistocene. Eventually it moved out over parts of North America and Europe, about 1.6 million years ago. No one knows what started the spread of the ice, but it might have had something to do with the way that the earth faces the sun.

The great freezing rivers of ice, called **glaciers**, moved slowly south. These heavy rivers of ice wore down the rocks underneath into great, smooth-sided valleys. These can still be seen today in different parts of Canada, the northern United States, and northern Europe.

The first ice age ended after a few thousand years when the climate became warmer and the ice melted. Then the ice advanced again about 900,000 years ago, and melted a few thousand years afterward. This happened three more times — the last advance of the ice ended only 11,000 years ago. At the moment, we may be living in a period between ice ages, and another one may happen in the future.

100,000
200,000
300,000
400,000
500,000
600,000
700,000
800,000
900,000
1 million years ago

The chart above shows the four ice ages of the last million years, with the warm spells in between.

Deep ice sheets spread out from the North Pole to cover much of Canada, the northern United States, northern Europe, and Asia. Separate ice sheets spread out from the Alps in Europe, and the Himalayas in Asia. These huge blocks of ice would have dwarfed the tallest skyscraper building.

106

Left: large woolly mammoths plodded across the icy Pleistocene lands. They were sometimes hunted by early humans. Dozens of deep-frozen mammoths have been dug up in Russia, and brave volunteers have found that their flesh is still good enough to eat. The baby mammoth called "Dima," shown above, was found in 1977.

Life in the cold

As the climate became colder, the plants slowly changed and the forests of oak and birch trees died out. Only pine trees and other conifers could survive. Animals that were used to warmer conditions moved southward. Many birds and mammals learned to cope with the new colder conditions by growing thicker feathers or fur. There were hares, wolves, reindeer, musk-oxen, and bears in the great northern ice fields of North America and Europe. These animals still live in northern Canada and Scandinavia. Other animals that evolved to live in cold conditions are no longer with us, such as the woolly rhinoceros that was covered by a coat of long, shaggy hair. The North American mastodon also developed a thick hairy coat to keep out the cold. And, of course, there were the mammoths.

Woolly mammoths

Great herds of woolly mammoths stalked across the frozen wastes of northern Europe and Russia. They were closely related to the living Indian elephant but had a thick coat of reddish hair. The mammoth had a high domed head and long coiled tusks. We know a great deal about woolly mammoths because many hundreds of skeletons have been collected. Even more dramatic are the flesh-and hair-covered mammoths that have been found in the icy ground of northern Russia.

107

In warmer times

During the warm years between the ice ages, life returned to normal in Europe and North America. There were oak trees, beech trees, lush grasses, flowers, and bushes with berries and fruits. The woolly mammoths and rhinos moved northward with the ice, and the animals that had retreated south now moved back.

In Europe there were straight-tusked elephants, woodland bison, giant cattle, hippos, cave lions, brown bears, and hyenas. The giant Irish deer was one of the more remarkable of these animals. It had huge antlers measuring up to 10 feet across.

In North America, many of the mammals have been beautifully preserved in the La Brea tar pits in California. These were sticky pools of oil that had seeped up through the rocks. Mammoths, bison, horses, and giant ground sloths fell into the tar and could not struggle out again. Their cries of fear attracted all kinds of meat-eaters, such as wolves and saber-toothed cats. These in turn fell into the tar and were killed.

On this page: straight-tusked elephants, woodland bison, cave lions, and giant deer all lived in Europe during the warm spells of the Pleistocene. The rhinoceroses moved northward as the ice retreated. On the opposite page: mammoths, giant sloths, wolves, and saber-toothed cats all meet a sticky death in the La Brea tar pits.

Straight-tusked elephant

Giant deer

Bison

Rhinoceros

Cave lion

Giant wombats and big birds

Life was very different in Australia and New Zealand during these times. There were no ice sheets in the south, so cold-loving animals did not appear. The mammals of Australia were all marsupials like the giant kangaroo *Procoptodon* and the wombat *Diprotodon*.

Life in New Zealand was even stranger. There were no mammals at all, and birds were the largest animals. Most important were the flightless **moas** that reached a height of 11 feet. These distant relatives of ostriches lived until quite recently, and they may have been wiped out by human hunters.

The giant kangaroo Procoptodon *and the marsupial "lion"* Thylacoleo *lived in Australia. In New Zealand, the huge flightless moas ruled the land.*

7. The First People

Our ape ancestors

We can find out a great deal about the first human beings by looking at the fossils of the skeletons and bones they left behind. But we can learn even more about our ancestors if we go further back in time and study the origins of our closest living relatives — the apes.

The primates

About 65 million years ago, at the time when the dinosaurs were dying out, the small, squirrellike *Plesiadapis* grubbed for insects in the Paleocene woods. This animal was one of the earliest **primates** — the group to which human beings belong.

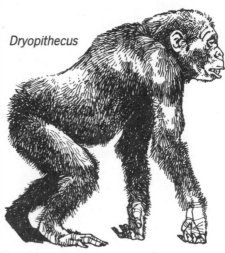

Dryopithecus

Above: Dryopithecus *may have been the first ape. It still had a monkeylike body, but its large apelike head contained a large and intelligent brain. It had no tail, and probably ran on all fours.*

Left: the long tail of this West African monkey cannot be used for hanging in trees — this is something that only their South American relatives have evolved to do.

110

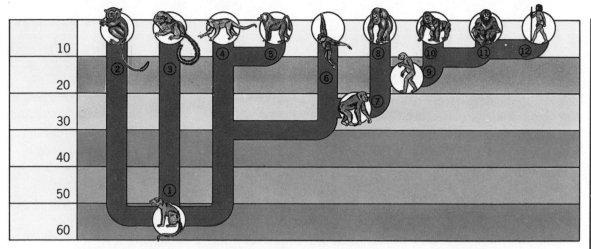

Primates include a great range of animals, such as apes and monkeys. The early primates, like *Plesiadapis*, probably looked like the long-tailed lemurs and tarsiers that live today. These small animals have large brains and strong hands that can carry out delicate tasks.

About 50 million years ago, in the middle of the Eocene, the first true monkeys appeared. Divided by the South Atlantic, the monkeys in South America evolved differently from their cousins in Africa and Asia. The South American monkeys had long tails that could be used like a fifth leg to hang from tree branches. The African monkeys are still around today, and they gave rise to the first apes in the Miocene.

There are only four kinds of apes alive today — the gibbons and orangutans of Asia, and the gorillas and chimps of Africa. Unlike monkeys, apes have no tail at all. Instead, they swing through the trees on their long dangling arms. About six or seven million years ago, at the end of the Miocene, a fifth kind of ape came on the scene. This was the human being.

Key to primate evolution:
1 *Plesiadapis*
2 Tarsier
3 Marmoset
4 Diana monkey
5 Baboon
6 Gibbon
7 *Dryopithecus*
8 Orangutan
9 *Ramapithecus*
10 Gorilla
11 Chimpanzee
12 Human being

Right: the chimpanzee, shown here in thoughtful mood. This highly intelligent ape is probably our closest living relative. Chimps live in the forests of central Africa, where they feed on fruits, nuts, leaves, and the occasional piece of meat.

111

The first humans

The first fossilized human skeletons come from rocks that are just under four million years old, although there are clues that humans might have branched off from the African apes six or seven million years ago. These early human fossils all come from Africa.

In 1974, Don Johanson discovered a remarkably well-preserved skeleton in rocks dated at 3 – 3.6 million years old in Ethiopia. It was nicknamed "Lucy" because it turned out to be the body of a young woman. Lucy had long legs, and she clearly walked upright. However, she had an ape-sized brain, and her teeth were still like those of an ape. Lucy was probably just over 3 feet tall. She belongs to the species called *Australopithecus afarensis*, which means "southern ape from Afar, Ethiopia."

In 1976, Mary Leakey discovered a trail of several dozen human footprints made in a layer of mud in Tanzania. The rocks are dated as being 3.75 million years old, and prove that humans were walking around even before Lucy was born.

Humans arrive
The human story begins 15 million years ago. At this time, there were many kinds of primitive apes living in the forests of Africa. As climates changed, the forests

Australopithecus lived in Africa two million years ago. These early humans still had apelike faces, but their brains had grown a little larger. They could walk fully upright, and they might have been able to use sticks and bones as tools or weapons.

JAWS

The jaw of *Australopithecus* is midway between the jaw of a modern ape and a modern human. *Australopithecus* did not have the large fangs that apes have today, but its other teeth were still large.

Ape

Australopithecus

Modern human

became smaller and most of the eastern part of Africa turned into dry grassland. There were now only forests in the western central area.

The early apes that were left in these forests evolved into the chimps and gorillas of today. The other apes in eastern Africa had to either adapt to a life out in the open or die. They evolved to stand upright, which allowed them to look out over the long grass for lions, and also to carry food in their arms. For a long time, scientists thought that the first human feature to evolve was the large brain. This does not seem to be correct now — walking upright came first.

Australopithecus afarensis is the oldest known species of human. Other species of *Australopithecus* are also known from Africa, and they lived up to about one million years ago. These later species were larger than Lucy, but they were still smaller than modern humans.

Is this the oldest human fossil? This trail of footprints from Tanzania, dated at 3.75 million years ago, proves that there were humans around. Only humans walk upright on the soles of their feet. These prints might have been made by an Australopithecus *like Lucy from Ethiopia.*

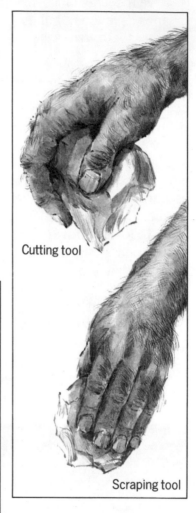

Homo habilis *may have been the first human being who ever made tools. They were made by chipping away at pieces of hard stone until they had sharp edges. Tool-making like this needs high intelligence.*

Cutting tool

Scraping tool

The early stone tools were very simple. They fitted easily into the hand, and had different edges for cutting or scraping. They may have been used to prepare the flesh of animals for eating.

Learning to use tools

Australopithecus died out a million years ago. Already, however, "true" humans had arrived on the scene. The first of the new species was *Homo habilis*, or "handy man," who first lived in Africa two million years ago.

Skulls of *Homo habilis* were found in 1964 in the Olduvai Gorge in Kenya. Although the pieces of bone are very incomplete, it has been worked out that these new people had much bigger brains than *Australopithecus*. They were still quite small, being only about 4 feet tall, but they mark a major step in human evolution. From this time onward, human brains became bigger and bigger.

It is very strange for us to imagine what life was like in Africa two million years ago, when there were two or three species of *Australopithecus* and one or more species of *Homo habilis* living side by side. No one can say how all these prehistoric humans got on with each other, but there is no evidence that they ever fought.

Fossils of stone tools have been found near the bones of *Homo habilis*, suggesting that "handy man" was the first tool maker. His greater intelligence and skill might also have allowed him to hunt better and to find more food than *Australopithecus*, and this may explain why the earlier type of human died out.

Missing links and dragon bones

The next human species — *Homo erectus*, or "upright man" — first lived in Africa about one million years ago. *Homo erectus* was larger than *Homo habilis*, being about 5 feet tall and stockily built. These people still had rather primitive faces with no chin and heavy bony ridges over the eyebrows. However, their brains were only slightly smaller than the brains of a modern human.

Homo erectus spread out all over the world from Africa. In 1891, a Dutch scientist called Eugene Dubois found a thigh bone and the top of a skull in Java, Southeast Asia. The skull cap of "Java man" showed that he had a brain that was nearly as big as that of a modern human. The leg bone was even more human in shape. When he brought these finds back to Europe, many scientists refused to believe that these ancient bones could have belonged to a human being.

The next *Homo erectus* discovery came from China. For many years, Chinese people had used medicine made from ground-up "dragon bones." Some of the "dragon bones" were actually the fossilized teeth of prehistoric human beings. They were traced to a large cave in Dragon's Hill outside Peking, where 14 skulls were dug up between 1923 and 1936. Fossils in the cave show that "Peking man" was a skilled hunter, and that he could make fires in order to cook his meat.

Homo erectus *is known from many parts of the world. In China, "Peking man" lived in caves and made a variety of tools for hunting. He also made fires for cooking the meat. This is shown by layers of ash in the caves.*

Modern humans arrive

By the time *Homo erectus* had died out, the last human species had arrived and taken over the world. This was *Homo sapiens*, or "wise man" — the group to which we belong today. One of our early relatives was Neanderthal man, who lived in Europe until about 35,000 years ago.

The first skeleton of Neanderthal man was found in the Neander Valley in Germany in 1857. The skeleton was deformed by disease, but the discoverers did not know that. For a long time, scientists thought that Neanderthal man was a dreadful dim-witted brute. They believed he walked around in a crouched position with his shoulders bent and his head looking down — the classic "cave man" that you still see in cartoons and films.

Neanderthal man had a heavier skull than living humans, but his brain was just as big, if not bigger! He walked fully upright, and made excellent tools. Far from being a brute, he was able to make carvings of the animals he saw around him in stone and bone. Tribes of these early people lived in Europe during the later ice ages, when their short stocky bodies helped to keep out the cold. They sheltered in caves, and made themselves warm clothing out of animal skins.

Modern *Homo sapiens* lived at the same time as Neanderthal man, but in warmer parts of the world such as North Africa and the Middle East. As the ice sheets melted, modern humans spread out into Europe and Asia

Neanderthal hunters wore animal skins to keep out the cold. They made good stone tools and weapons, and lived in caves or huts. These people were very like us, although they were slightly more heavily built.

and gradually took over from the Neanderthals. In Europe, the Neanderthals moved north, following the retreating herds of mammoths and reindeer that they fed on. Some of them might have joined the tribes of modern humans as well.

The modern humans made better tools than the Neanderthals, as well as beautiful paintings and carvings. After the end of the last ice age, about 11,000 years ago, the people living in the Middle East began to farm their land. This meant that humans settled down in one place instead of wandering around in search of food. They built themselves houses, which led to the first villages and towns. As trading between villages started, languages became more complicated and different people became skilled at making pots or tools. Civilization had arrived.

About 20,000 years ago, modern humans lived in caves or huts made from wood and animal skins. They used skillfully made tools of stone or bone to prepare their food, or to make clothing.

A cave painting of a bison from the Lascaux caves in France. These beautiful paintings were produced by modern humans in stone age times.

Ramapithecus	Australopithecus	Homo habilis	Homo erectus	Neanderthal man	Modern human
15 million years ago. Africa, Asia	1–4 million years ago. Africa	1.5–2 million years ago. Africa	0.1–1.5 million years ago. Africa, Asia, Europe	35,000–100,000 years ago. Europe	Since 100,000 years ago. Worldwide

The scale of life

The story of human life has taken just 15 million years, beginning with the appearance of the apelike *Ramapithecus* in Africa. *Ramapithecus* was followed by *Australopithecus* four million years ago, *Homo habilis* appeared two million years ago, and *Homo erectus* one million years ago. Neanderthals and modern humans only came onto the scene about 100,000 years ago.

Human beings do not look very impressive when they are compared with some of the huge animals that have lived in the past. Are humans more successful than the dinosaurs were in their day?

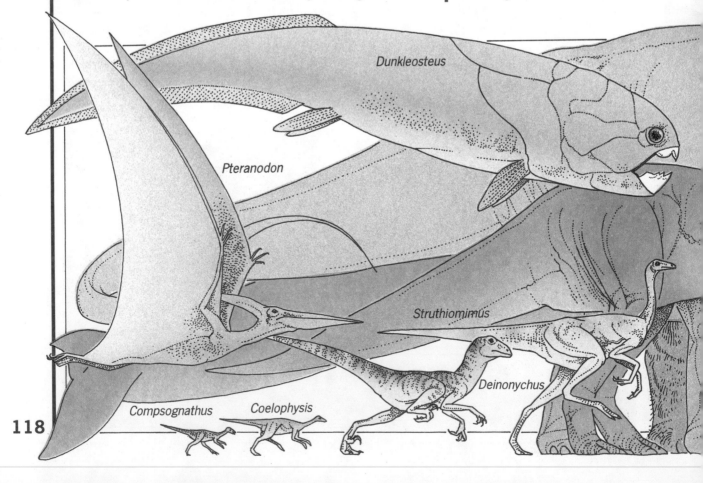

If the whole history of life on earth is compared to a single year, it might be easier to understand what a short amount of time this really is. Imagine that life arose at the beginning of January. Life in the sea became common near the end of September. Fish appeared in October, amphibians and reptiles in November, and mammals at the beginning of December. Mammals only became important late in December, and humans just appear fleetingly in the evening of December 31.

How have human beings become so successful in such a short space of time? It is certainly not because we are particularly big or powerful — we would have been dwarfed by most of the dinosaurs, and many of the other huge beasts that ruled the earth in the past. We are tiny compared to the great whale that lives in the oceans today, and much smaller than the biggest living land mammals.

The key to our success lies in our large brains and intelligence. We can live in all parts of the world because we can make clothing, grow large amounts of food, and control nature in a way that no other animal has ever been able to do before us.

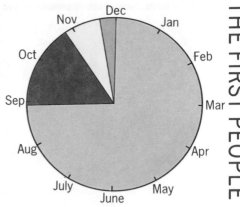

If the history of life were seen as a single year, then early life in the sea began late in September. Life moved onto land in November, mammals appeared in December, and humans only managed to squeeze in on the evening of December 31.

Rhamphorynchus

Apatosaurus

Baluchitherium

Iguanodon

Moa

Archaeopteryx

Blue whale

Human

Dryopithecus

Struthiosaurus

Glyptodon

Glossary

Ammonite ("ram's-horn") A coiled shell-fish of the Mesozoic, related to the modern squid and octopus.

Ammonoid A coiled shellfish. A large group that includes the AMMONITES.

Amphibian ("two-lives") A backboned animal that lives both on land and in the water, for example a frog or a salamander.

Ankylosaur ("crooked-reptile") An armored dinosaur with a covering of bony plates on its back and a knobby tail.

Apodan ("no-feet") A small wormlike AMPHIBIAN that has lost its legs and lives by burrowing in the damp soil.

Archosaur ("ruling-reptile") A REPTILE, such as a crocodile, dinosaur, THECODONTIAN, or PTEROSAUR.

Bacteria ("small-stick") Simple, microscopic creatures that are made up from single CELLS. These cells are often stick-shaped.

Belemnite ("dart-stone") A bullet-shaped shell found inside the body of a squidlike shellfish. Found in Jurassic and Cretaceous rocks.

Brachiopod ("arm-foot") A primitive type of shelled animal that was common in ancient seas, but is much rarer today. Each of its two shells are different shapes.

Brontothere ("thunder-beast") Massive horned MAMMAL of the Eocene and Oligocene.

Carnivore ("flesh-eater") An animal that lives by eating other animals rather than by eating plants.

Carnosaur ("flesh-eating-reptile") A large meat-eating dinosaur, such as *Tyrannosaurus* or *Allosaurus*.

The Cretaceous carnosaur *Baryonyx walkeri*

Cells ("small-space") The basic units that make up all living things.

Ceratopsian ("horned-face") A plant-eating dinosaur with horns on its snout and face. Examples are *Protoceratops* and *Triceratops*.

Chalicothere ("cup-beast") Plant-eating MAMMAL that lived between the Eocene and Pliocene (such as *Moropus*).

Coelacanth ("hollow-spine") LOBE-FINNED fish that has lived from the Carboniferous to the present day.

Cold-blooded An animal, like a REPTILE, AMPHIBIAN, or fish, that cannot control its body temperature as we can.

Cynodont ("dog-tooth") MAMMALLIKE REPTILE of the Triassic period. Cynodonts had doglike teeth with pointed fangs.

Deinonychosaur ("terrible-clawed-reptile") Meat-eating dinosaur that lived in Cretaceous times. Deinonychosaurs had large scythelike claws on their hind feet that they used to attack their prey.

Dicynodont ("two-dog-teeth") One of the plant-eating MAMMALLIKE REPTILES of Permian and Triassic times, such as *Lystrosaurus*. Dicynodonts often had only two teeth, each with a pointed edge.

Dinocephalian ("terrible-headed") A MAMMALLIKE REPTILE of the late Permian. Some fed on plants, and some on animals.

Edentate ("toothless") A South American MAMMAL with small teeth, or no teeth at all. Examples include anteaters and sloths.

Elasmosaur ("plate-reptile") A long-necked sea REPTILE that lived in the seas during Cretaceous times.

Evolution ("unfolding") The development of plants and animals over a long period of time. Animals and plants *evolve* as a result of changes in their living conditions, and in each other.

Extinction ("wiping-out") The death of a SPECIES.

Fossil ("dug-up") The remains of plants and animals that once lived on the earth.

Geological time The hundreds of millions of years that make up the history of the earth and the history of life.

Geologist ("earth-expert") A scientist who studies rocks and the history of the earth.

Glacier ("ice") A moving "river" of ice.

Gorgonopsian ("gorgon-face") A meat-eating MAMMALLIKE REPTILE of the late Permian.

Hadrosaur ("big-reptile") A plant-eating dinosaur of the late Cretaceous. Because of their broad flat snouts, Hadrosaurs are often known as "duckbilled" dinosaurs.

Ichthyosaur ("fish-reptile") A dolphin-shaped REPTILE that lived in Mesozoic seas at the same time that dinosaurs ruled the earth.

Labyrinthodont ("labyrinth-tooth") An early AMPHIBIAN of the Carboniferous.

Lens The front part of the eye that takes in light and focuses it.

Lepospondyl A small Carboniferous AMPHIBIAN. Many looked like modern-day salamanders. One example is *Diplocaulus*.

Lobe-fin A fish with fleshy fins, such as the LUNG FISH and the COELACANTH. These fish are closely related to the AMPHIBIANS.

Lung fish A fish that can breathe underwater with its gills like an ordinary fish, but can also breathe in air with its lungs.

Mammal A WARM-BLOODED animal with hair that produces milk to feed its young. Examples include mice, rabbits, cats, dogs, elephants, and humans.

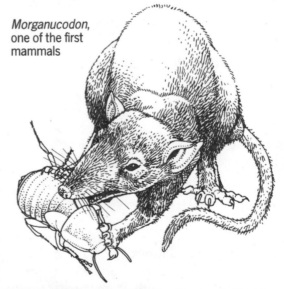

Morganucodon, one of the first mammals

Mammallike reptile A REPTILE of the Permian or Triassic that was related to the ancestors of the MAMMALS.

Marsupial ("pouched") A MAMMAL that bears live young which develop in a pouch on the mother's body. Examples include kangaroos, wombats, and koalas in Australia, and opossums in South America.

Mass extinction When many plants and animals died out at the same time.

Missing link A popular name for an unknown FOSSIL creature that is halfway between two other SPECIES.

Moa A large FOSSIL bird from the Pleistocene of New Zealand. Moas could not fly, and they were hunted to EXTINCTION by early humans.

Moa

Monotreme A MAMMAL that lays eggs. The only living monotremes are the platypus and echidna of Australia and New Guinea.

Mosasaur ("Maas-reptile") Giant fish-eating lizard of the Cretaceous seas. FOSSILS were found near the River Maas in the Netherlands.

Nautiloid ("sailor") A coiled shellfish, related to the AMMONOIDS. Nautiloids have lived from the Devonian to the present day.

Nothosaur ("southern-reptile") These sea REPTILES of the Triassic included the ancestors of the PLESIOSAURS.

Ornithischian ("bird-hip") A major group of dinosaurs that had a birdlike hip area. The ornithischians were all plant-eaters, and included *Iguanodon* and *Stegosaurus*.

Ornithopod ("bird-foot") A plant-eating ORNITHISCHIAN dinosaur, such as *Iguanodon* and the HADROSAURS.

Ostracoderm ("shell-skin") Primitive jawless fish, covered in bony armor.

Paleontologist ("expert-on-ancient-life") A scientist who studies FOSSILS and the history of life.

Pareiasaur An ugly plant-eating REPTILE of the late Permian, with a massive horned head and skin covered with bony warts and scales.

Placental A MAMMAL that gives birth to fully developed young. Most mammals are placentals, such as mice, dogs, horses, whales, and humans.

Placoderm ("platy-skin") A primitive fish of the Silurian or Devonian periods with bony plates over the head area.

Placodont ("platy-tooth") A marine REPTILE of the Triassic that fed on shellfish, which it crushed with its flat teeth.

Plesiosaur ("near-reptile") A sea REPTILE with a long neck and four flippers that lived in the Jurassic and Cretaceous seas.

Pliosaur ("more-reptile") A large, short-necked PLESIOSAUR of the Jurassic or Cretaceous.

Prehistoric Something that dates from before "history" (that is, before the invention of writing).

Primate ("first") A MAMMAL of the group that includes monkeys, apes, and humans. It is called the "first" group because it is our own.

The early primate *Dryopithecus*

Pronghorn An antelopelike animal with a forked, or pronglike, horn on its snout.

Prosauropod A plant-eating dinosaur that lived before the SAUROPODS in late Triassic and early Jurassic times, and which includes *Plateosaurus*.

Pterosaur ("winged-reptile") A flying REP-TILE of the Mesozoic, related to the di-nosaurs and the THECODONTIANS.

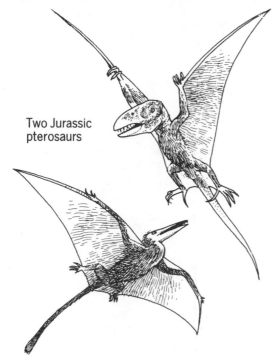

Two Jurassic pterosaurs

Reptile ("crawler") A COLD-BLOODED animal covered with scales. Examples in-clude lizards, snakes, crocodiles, turtles, and dinosaurs.

Rhynchosaur ("beaked-reptile") A plant-eating REPTILE with a hooked beak that lived in Triassic times.

Rodent ("gnawer") A small MAMMAL that feeds on tough plants by gnawing. Ex-amples are mice, rats, beavers, and por-cupines.

Sail-backed reptile An early Permian MAM-MALLIKE REPTILE that usually had a "sail" made from skin and bone along its back.

Saurischian ("lizard-hip") This major group of dinosaurs had a "lizardlike" hip region. They included both meat-eaters and plant-eaters.

Sauropod ("reptile-foot") A large plant-eating dinosaur with a long neck and a long tail, like *Diplodocus* or *Apatosaurus*. Lived in the Jurassic and Cretaceous.

Skeleton The bony framework that holds up the bodies of fish, AMPHIBIANS, REPTILES, birds, and MAMMALS.

Species The basic "kinds" of plants and animals. All of the members of a species look similar and can breed together. Human beings form one species, alligators form another, and so on.

Stegosaur ("plated-reptile") A plant-eating dinosaur with plates or spines along its back. Lived in Jurassic and Cretaceous times.

Stromatolite ("blanket-stone") A mound of simple single-celled creatures built up in layers, with layers of mud in between.

Thecodontian ("socketed-teeth") The early ARCHOSAUR group, which includes the ancestors of dinosaurs, PTEROSAURS, and crocodiles. They were among the first ani-mals to have each tooth set in its own socket, or hole, in the jaw bone.

Toxodont ("arched-tooth") A large plant-eating MAMMAL that lived between Oligocene and Pleistocene times in South America. The upper grinding teeth had an arched shape.

Trilobite ("three-segments") An animal with many legs that was common on the seabed between Cambrian and Silurian times. It had a tough body covering that was divided into three sections.

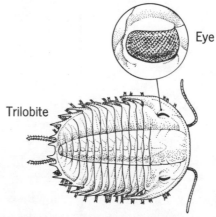

Eye

Trilobite

Uintathere ("Uinta beast") A large horned plant-eating MAMMAL of the Eocene and Oligocene. First discovered in the Uinta Mountains of Utah.

Warm-blooded An animal that can control its body temperature to a certain level, such as a bird or a MAMMAL.

Index

Page numbers in *italics* refer to pictures

Acknowledgments

2 F.M. Carpenter, Museum of Comparative Zoology; **11** (top) Mansell Collection; **12** (bottom) Yale Peabody Museum of Natural History; **13** (top) Dinosaur National Monument, Utah; **15** (top) **16** (bottom left) Imitor; **17** (top) Jenny Chapman, (bottom) Imitor; **18** (top) Mansell Collection, (bottom) Peale Museum, Baltimore; **25** (bottom) Imitor; **32** (top) By James Amos © 1985 National Geographic Society; **34** (bottom) National Galleries of Scotland; **35** Peter Scoones/Seaphot; **37** (bottom) Colin Caket/ZEFA; **38** (bottom) Dept. of Geology, National Museum of Wales; **42** (bottom) Imitor; **69** (top) By James Amos © 1985 National Geographic Society; **76** (bottom) **78** (middle) Imitor; **81** (top) Museum of Comparative Zoology, Cambridge, Mass.; **85** (bottom) Museum of Natural History, Berlin; **103** (top) E & P Bauer/ZEFA; **111** (bottom) P. Morris; **113** (bottom) Photograph by John Reader; **116** (top) 'M. Ruspoli/© C.N.M.H.S./S.P.A.D.E.M.'.